T0001663

CRETE

Travel with Marco Polo
Insider Tips

INSIDER TIP
Your shortcut
to a great
experience

MARCO POLO
TOP HIGHLIGHTS

CHANIÁ OLD TOWN ⭐
This is Crete in a nutshell: history and joie de vivre, art and good Mediterranean cuisine in between high mountain ranges and the Aegean Sea.
📷 *Tip: At dusk, step onto one of the boats at the Janissary Mosque and take your pictures from the water!*

➤ p. 42 Chaniá

ELAFONÍSI BEACH ⭐
The white sand and turquoise sea are reminiscent of the South Pacific, and the shallow water makes it a perfect beach for children.

➤ p. 52 Chaniá

VENETIAN HARBOUR ⭐3
At Crete's most beautiful harbour front, in Réthimno's old town, Maria's Knossós taverna serves delicious freshly caught fish.
📷 *Tip: The harbour is at its most picturesque when the lights come on in the evening and the crumbling render becomes almost unnoticeable.*

➤ p. 60 Réthimno

ARKÁDI MONASTERY ⭐
Freedom or death? In this Venetian monastery, the besieged Cretans gave the Ottomans a gruesome answer to the question.
📷 *Tip: Drive 500 m in the direction of Klissídi for the best views of the monastery.*

➤ p. 67 Réthimno

MÁTALA 🎯 8

To this day, the former fishing village and hippie paradise still has a very special charm.

📷 *Tip: The wide-angle view from inside one of the caves provides an excellent frame for your photos.*

➤ p. 86 Iráklio

PRÉVELI 🎯

This beach cannot be accessed by road, but a stream runs across the sand and you can admire a palm grove in the red canyon behind it. Furthermore, there are two monasteries and a lovely ancient bridge.

➤ p. 70 Réthimno

LASSÍTHI PLATEAU 🎯 9

Are you longing for the simple country life? On Crete's largest high-altitude plain you will find exactly that.

📷 *Tip: If you meet a flock of sheep on the road, very carefully drive right into the middle of it and take pictures from the side window.*

➤ p. 101 Ágios Nikólaos & around

ARCHAEOLOGICAL MUSEUM 🎯 6

In Crete's treasure trove in Iráklio you can learn how the Minoans lived, what they believed in and what was beautiful to them.

➤ p. 76 Iráklio

KNOSSÓS 🎯

There is a lot to see in the ruins of this 3,500-year-old major city which brings archaeology to life.

➤ p. 82 Iráklio

SPINALÓNGA 🎯 10

Eerily beautiful: up until 60 years ago, the lepers of Crete used to live on this fortified island.

➤ p. 99 Ágios Nikólaos & around

CONTENTS

CONTENTS

⏱	Plan your visit	🍴	Eating/drinking	☂	Rainy day activities
€–€€€	Price categories	🛍	Shopping		Budget activities
(*)	Premium-rate phone number	🍸	Going out		Family activities
		🏖	Top beaches	⚑	Classic experiences

(🗺 A2) Refers to the removable pull-out map
(0) Located off the map

BEST OF
CRETE

It's hard to imagine a more idyllic scene than the lagoon at Bálos Beach

BEST ☂

WHEN IT RAINS

ACTIVITIES TO BRIGHTEN YOUR DAY

JUST DIVE IN
Rainy days are ideal for scuba diving – children can learn with special equipment in the hotel pool and adults in the open sea – try the *Atlantis Diving Centre* near Réthimno.
➤ p. 33, Sport & activities

POTTERY VILLAGE
Margarítes is home to more than 20 pottery studios that are clustered so close together that it doesn't even matter if it rains. There's often a delightful symbiosis of the artistic and the useful – and the items don't cost the earth.
➤ p. 68, Réthimno

LOVELY TO TOUCH
If you can overcome your fear, you'll quickly discover that handling snakes can be a pleasure. You can stroke the pythons at *Reptisland* in Melidóni. They are guaranteed not to be hungry.
➤ p. 68, Réthimno

SHAKE IT UP
You wouldn't want to experience a real earthquake, but if you're interested to know what it feels like, try the *earthquake simulator* at the *Natural History Museum* in Iráklio. It quakes every 30 minutes.
➤ p. 79, Iráklio

MARINE LIFE
When it is raining, visit Greece's most modern aquarium. There are over 2,500 creatures in the *Cretaquarium* (photo) in Goúrnes, among them octopus, lobsters, seahorses and sharks.
➤ p. 80, Iráklio

DESCEND INTO THE UNDERWORLD
Descend 550m into a fantastical world of stalagmites and stalactites in the *Sventóni stalactite cave* on the edge of Zonianá and discover the beautiful forms created by water.
➤ p. 85, Iráklio

BEST 🐷
ON A BUDGET

FOR SMALLER WALLETS

ADMISSION FREE
Admission to all the excavation sites and archaeological museums on Crete is free on 6 March, 18 April, 18 May as well as the last weekend in September and 28 October each year. It's also free on the first Sunday of each month between November and March.

WHERE THE OLIVE OIL FLOWS
The young proprietor of the *Paráskákis* olive oil factory will show you the secrets of harvesting olive oil, and you can also go on a free guided tour of the ultra-modern facility in Melidóni.
➤ p. 68, Réthimno

FREE ADMISSION TO THE POOL
Admission prices into waterparks are usually extremely expensive but you can enter the *Star Beach Water Park* in Liménas Chersónisou for free. You only pay to ride the slides.
➤ p. 83, Iráklio

RUINS IN AN OLIVE GROVE
After seeing the Odéon and Títus Basilica of Górtis, many miss out on a lovely walk through the ruins of the Roman city in age-old olive groves, which, unlike the excavations on the opposite side of the road – are free of charge (photo).
➤ p. 89, Iráklio

BY BUS INSTEAD OF CAR
There is an excellent public bus network on Crete which connects almost all villages on the island. Prices are low: from as little as 1.80 euros you can get to the nearest beach by bus. You may think about saving yourself the expense of a hire car.
➤ p. 141, Good to know

FREE CONCERTS
Admission to all the concerts held at the four-day *Houdétsi Festival* of Cretan music is free for visitors.
➤ p. 143, Iráklio

BEST WITH CHILDREN

FUN FOR YOUNG & OLD

EXPENSIVE, BUT GREAT FUN

Parents and two children will have to part with at least 130 euros at the *Aqua Creta Limnoúpolis* leisure pool near Chaniá. If this doesn't put you off, then you can enjoy the five water slides (up to 55m high), the Crazy and Lazy River and the pools for all ages as often as you like.

➤ p. 46, Chaniá

TAKE A MINI TRAIN

Puffa puff – here comes the train! And although it's not a full-sized train that rolls along proper tracks, it does have a *motorised engine* with three open carriages and it rides along many of the streets on rubber tyres. Check out the train timetable in Georgioúpoli.

➤ p. 50, Chaniá

SAILING WITH PIRATES

Have Lego pirates taken over your bedroom at home? Then it's high time to treat your children to a trip on the *Barbarossa* pirate ship. It is moored in Réthimno harbour and is waiting for a crew of little sailors.

➤ p. 64, Réthimno

DINOSAUR ENCOUNTERS

There are no living dinosaurs on Crete, but the show in the *Dinosauria Park* in Goúrnes is extremely well presented. You'll see 30 types of dinosaur in 4 acres, moving in 3D on the screen. There's even a dinosaur hospital where you can watch a dinosaur hatch.

➤ p. 80, Iráklio

BEST 🏴

CLASSIC EXPERIENCES

ONLY ON CRETE

THE SOUND OF LYRES IN CHANIÁ

The *lýra* and *laoúto* are Crete's traditional musical instruments. Every night you can hear them being played in the modern *ouzerí Chalkína* in Chaniá's old town, for locals and foreign guests. The lyrics are mostly about love and the fight for freedom.

➤ p. 47, Chaniá

RAKÍ & MEZÉDES

When *mezédes* (photo) are served, your table will be laden with a variety of small dishes. As an accompaniment, Cretans love to drink *rakí* from small decanters. The ideal venue for this is a *rakádika*; there are a number of them squeezed into the Odós Vernárdou in Réthimno.

➤ p. 63, Réthimno

NIGHTLIFE IN IRÁKLIO

In the street cafés surrounding the *Platía Korái,* mostly young Cretans sit on funky lounge furniture, meet their friends and listen to music. Iced coffee is the most popular drink.

➤ p. 81, Iráklio

SURROUNDED BY MOUNTAINS

Uninhabited plateaux are a geographical feature of the island. During the summer countless sheep and goats graze here, and during the winter they are covered in snow. The *Nída Plateau,* just under the summit of Mount Psilorítis, is easy to reach and beautiful to stroll through.

➤ p. 85, Iráklio

BACK TO THE HIPPIES

Mátala became famous in the 1960s, when hippies came from all over the world to live here. Every year around Whitsun, the spirit of Woodstock is rekindled during the *Mátala Beach Festival.* The stage is set up on the beach, with a campsite right behind it. The music unites all generations.

➤ p. 143, Festivals & events

GET TO KNOW CRETE

Octopus drying in Chaniá harbour

DISCOVER CRETE

Inland Crete, with its villages and monasteries, is as varied as the island's coastline

Approaching Crete from the air, it becomes obvious that this island is essentiallly a vast, high mountain range in the middle of the sea. Its beaches are more of a sideshow, and only a few paces inland you begin to discover one of the most unspoilt and varied islands in Europe.

UNSPOILT VILLAGES

Don't miss the southern part of the island, where the old fort of Frangokastéllo stands guard over a wide sandy beach. From here, a narrow road winds up the steep slope like the thread of a corkscrew. A few houses are scattered down below, in the glowing sun on the coastal plain. Beyond, the sea doesn't reach land again until Libya. There is a touch of Africa in the air – and occasionally a little dust from the Sahara. A rustic *kafenió* dozes in the sun at the entrance to the first mountain village you come to. Danish landlady Janina speaks many languages. Her Cretan

1900–1450 BCE
Minoan era. Palaces of Knossós, Festós, Mália

1450–480 BCE
Greek tribes settle on Crete. About 100 independent city states are founded

480 BCE–CE 395
Classical, Hellenistic and Roman eras

395–1204
Byzantine era. Constantinople rules Crete

1204–1669
Venetian era

1669–1898
Ottoman era

1898–1913
Crete is autonomous

husband, Bábis, has decorated the airy terrace with goat skulls. The mountain tea is freshly brewed, and a lavender stalk floats on top of the carob lemonade. The home-made wine tastes of Cretan soil. Here in Kallikrátis it is not very difficult to forget about the rest of the world.

Continue to another mountain village: Anógia. It is still early in the year. In the modest coffee shop on the town square wood is crackling in the fireplace. Chairs with woven seats line three of the walls. Against the fourth wall, behind the counter, the host brews rich coffee in brass and copper pots, pours it into small espresso cups and serves it to the guests with a glass of water. Just above the counter is a huge flat-screen television broadcasting an important soccer match. Everyone is watching and commentating. Then the half-time whistle. A guest turns off the television. Two young men, both in OFI Iráklio shirts, each grab a *lýra*, an age-old Cretan instrument, and begin playing and singing masterfully. The essence of Crete fills the room. After 15 minutes, the television is turned on again and the music stops. An American fast-food chain advertises hamburgers, and then the soccer game continues.

MODERN TIMES

Time hasn't stood still on Crete. Gigantic wind turbines rotate on mountain ridges, and on the motorways and dual carriageways of the north coast, the Cretans rush from town to town. In Iráklio an EU institute takes care of data security for the whole of Europe, while on the south coast, Chinese investors want to build a large container ship port for the distribution of their wares in the Mediterranean and Black

1913
Union with liberated Greece

1941-1944
German occupation, guerrilla war

1944-1949
Greek civil war between leftists and conservative government forces

1967-1974
Military dictatorship

1981
Greece joins the European Union

2002
The euro replaces the drachma as currency

2010-2020
Greek financial crisis

seas. On the Lassíthi Plateau, Albanian migrant workers harvest organically grown potatoes and Pakistani shepherds phone home from the back of their donkey or the seat of their moped. Crete is now very much a part of the globalised world.

BOTH WILD & FRIENDLY

But Crete also has another interesting and distinctive side. Travelling from the airport, one cannot help but notice the bullet holes in the street signs which serve as target practice for many Cretans. Every shot is an expression of the locals' unease over too much state authority. This is very much an echo from their past under foreign rule: until Crete's union with Greece in 1912 and during the German occupation (1941–44) every act of resistance against the state authorities was seen as an act of bravery and is still praised in school text books. To this day the Cretan motto remains: "Freedom or death!"

Despite this rather wild behaviour Crete remains one of the safest holiday destinations in the world. For centuries, hospitality has been one of their priorities and as a visitor you will always experience it – certainly when you are away from the tourist centres. Rakí and fruit are served as dessert free of charge in most tavernas and the owner often invites guests to a cup of Greek coffee. And if you should stumble on a village wedding, you may well be invited to stay and join the celebrations.

FASCINATING TOWNS & VARIED BEACHES

Some 623,000 people live on the island and all the major towns are situated on the north coast. For visitors life is pretty laid back. Allow yourself to be beamed back 3,500 years, if only for a day, when you visit the Iráklio Archaeological Museum and the palace town of Knossós, just a few miles away. But it is not for Crete's ancient past alone that four million-plus visitors fly here every year. The main attractions are the beaches. Whether sand or shingle, the island has it all: some are miles long and some are backed with dunes. There are party beaches such as the one at Mália; tiny bays like those at Xerókambos, where no one minds how little you are wearing; beaches with rows of deck chairs and sun shades, bars and a water-sports station; and then there are more isolated strips of shingle or sand against steep cliffs and sandy slopes. None of the beaches are off-limits to visitors.

ADVENTURES FOR ACTIVE PEOPLE

Admittedly, you can find good beaches all over the world. However, there aren't many places where the mountains are as close to the sea as they are on Crete, enticing visitors away from the beach for other activities. There are over 100 unspoilt gorges to explore; stalactite caves to be discovered and 2,000-m mountains to be climbed. And wherever you go, all the traditional mountain villages have their *kafenía*, where interested locals will be happy to greet you.

AT A GLANCE

623,000
Population

Isle of Wight: 142,000

75 PEOPLE

per km²
Isle of Wight:
372 per km²

1,066 km
Coastline

Corsica: 1,000 km

8,261 km²
Area
Fourth largest island in the
Mediterranean

Mallorca: 3,640 km²

HIGHEST PEAK:
PSILORÍTIS

2,456 M

Ben Nevis: 1,345 m

WARMEST MONTHS

JULY
AND
AUGUST
37°C

MOST IMPORTANT
WORD IN GREEK

NE

Meaning "Yes" in
English

MOST FAMOUS CRETAN

Alexis Sorbás, hero of a novel (and subsequent movie hero — played
by Anthony Quinn) written by Cretan author Níkos Kazantzákis

IRÁKLIO

Biggest city, with 140,730 inhabitants

OLIVE OIL CONSUMPTION
25-30 litres per person
per year

PALM BEACHES?
Yes - at Vái and Préveli

UNDERSTAND CRETE

BYZANTINE

Do you like to understand what you are reading? On Crete, you'll see thousands of mostly brown signs with the English word "Byzantine" on them. The signs indicate the island's relics and remains from the Byzantine era, from around 500 to 1453 CE, so roughly the time of our Middle Ages. Crete belonged to the Byzantine Empire until 1204 CE. This empire covered all Asia Minor, the Balkans and Greece. The capital was Constantinople, renamed Istanbul after the Turks conquered it in 1453.

ANAGRAMS

Cretan signposts do not always stick to standard Greek spelling. And that can sometimes make foreigners despair. The names of many towns and villages may be spelt differently on signposts and maps. And even more so when it comes to the Latin alphabet. "*Agia*", for instance, which means "Saint", is sometimes "*Agía*" (as used by Marco Polo), at other times it's "*Aghia*" or "Ayia". All three versions are correct. If you don't have many rules, you won't make many mistakes. All we can do is be resourceful.

PLASTICULTURE

What's that glittering over there? Many of the island's coastal plains sparkle in the sun like vast lakes when you look down on them. This is due primarily to the Netherlands. It was a Dutchman who, in the early 1960s, showed the Cretans how to grow tomatoes, fruit and vegetables in greenhouses. Thanks to the Cretan sun, there's no need for expensive heating.

Although the farmers earn good money from the *thermokípia*, all the environment gets is rubbish. That's because the greenhouses are covered in plastic film rather than glass, and once that becomes useless, it is shredded by the wind and blows away.

KRÍSIS

The word "*krísis*" ("crisis" in English) refers to the country's ongoing financial woes, and has been on every Cretan's lips since 2010. It has become the normal state, indeed normal life. People are dealing with the tax increases and pension reductions, with the lack of work and future prospects.

Flower beds are being turned into vegetable plots, and people are heating more with wood than with oil or electricity. In the tavernas, unlike the "olden days", people are only ordering what they can eat. Instead of spending 93 minutes (which has been proven statistically!) over a cup of coffee, people are now spending three hours with it. And they are helping each other with the olive and grape harvests instead of employing Eastern Europeans. They'll get by – as long as the tourists keep coming.

STRANGE SOUNDS?

Young Cretans' taste in music is just as contemporary as that of young people in the rest of Europe. And yet, most of them are just as fascinated by *lýra* and *laoúto* as their grandparents were. The three-stringed pear-shaped lyre and the *laoúto*, a five-stringed plucked instrument, fills half of all of the music programmes on the radio, and can be heard in tavernas around the island. In fact, they even occasionally make it into the clubs.

Mostly the lyre players create a kind of monotonous speech song called *mantinádes* and *rizítika*. Although there are classics, texts are also often improvised for a specific situation and for those present. So if you're in a taverna and everyone suddenly turns around to look at you, it's quite possible that you're currently the subject of some gentle teasing.

SIDER TIP
Why is everybody looking at me?

SOAP OPERAS

Cretans love their favourite television programmes, mainly soaps, more and more of which are now being made in Greek. Viewers demand clever and sophisticated dialogues as well as topics, issues and dramas that are relevant to Greek people. The comedy series *Eptá thanássimes petherés* (Seven deadly mothers-in-law), for example, focuses on the lengths a mother will go to in order to keep her mummy's boy (or girl) all to herself. Remarkable proof of the trans-Aegean relationship is the huge success of a Turkish soap about Sultan Suleiman the Magnificent. Here, Cretans are beginning to respect a past ruler who once treated their ancestors very badly indeed.

CRETAN LEGENDS

Life was pretty exciting in the ancient world of the gods. One drama followed the next, and they were not always suitable for young eyes. Zeus, the father of the gods, abducted Europa, the underage daughter of the Phoenician king of Crete, and fathered *Mínos*, the island's first king, with her. Minos's wife *Pasiphae* burned with lust for a white bull. She had a life-like model of a cow made and concealed

There's no Cretan music without a *lýra*

herself inside it. The bull fell for this trick, and the queen conceived a hybrid child: the legendary minotaur.

Mínos had the beast locked up in a labyrinth, where it was regularly fed young Athenian men and virgins. The Athenian hero Theseus managed to kill the bull and, using Ariadne's thread, found his way out of the labyrinth. He took Ariadne home with him. But on a stopover on the island of Naxos, *Dionysos*, the god of wine and theatre, spotted the pretty Ariadne and immediately married her. Theseus continued without her, but set black sails. These were misinterpreted by his father, the Athenian King Aegeus, who then threw himself into the sea in despair. Since then, this sea has been called the Aegean Sea.

ENTÁXI & ENTÉCHNO

When a Cretan says *entáxi*, he is saying "ok" rather than asking for a taxi. *Entéchno* is a similar trap – and as a music style, is on everyone's lips. However, it has absolutely nothing to do with techno. *Entéchno* refers to rocky ballads with Greek texts, usually performed by a soloist accompanied by a guitar. And you don't have to be a techno freak to enjoy it.

Out and about with donkeys and ponies in the lush green hills of the *Psilorítis* mountains

RARELY ALONE

Cretans don't like being alone. Even spending time with one other person is only for romantic couples, otherwise *paréa* is the order of the day. Whether they're enjoying a coffee or a meal, dancing at a nightclub or going on holiday, Cretans like to socialise in large, companionable groups. And the question that is asked later is never about the quality of the hotel or food, but whether the *paréa* was good. On the rare occasions when people do have to be alone, they still have their saints. They are always present everywhere in the form of icons. And of course, they can also be found in the many churches, chapels and on numerous painted signs on the roadsides. It means that Cretans can rest assured that they're always well protected and in good company.

SCHNAPPS AS CULTURAL HERITAGE

If you want ouzo, you're in the wrong place. People drink *rakí* on Crete, which is distilled around the clock in October and November in hundreds of tiny distilleries in villages and olive groves. It is often made without additives, only from the fermented mash that is left over after the grapes have been pressed for wine. Guesthouses, holiday apartments and hotels frequently leave a small carafe of *rakí* in guests' rooms on arrival, and restaurants often give diners a free *rakí* with dessert, and sometimes even at breakfast.

They can afford to be generous with it, because to date the tax on the

TRUE OR FALSE?

ALL CRETANS LIVE A HEALTHY LIFESTYLE

The "Cretan diet" is generally regarded as one of the healthiest. This has also translated into healthy profits for many cookbook authors on the topic. It is true that research showed a connection between diet, a long life expectancy and a low incidence of heart attacks on Crete, but this research was done in the 1950s and 60s. At that time, most people on Crete had low incomes and could only afford fruit and vegetables, plenty of (small) fish and very little meat and animal fat. Today, this has radically changed, with many overweight children on the island indicating that now there is excessive fast-food consumption and sugar intake – and less of a Spartan diet.

Cretan national drink, which is very similar to Italian grappa, is very low. This is very much to the annoyance of the politicians in Brussels, who demand it should be taxed the same as ouzo and whisky. The Cretans are vehemently opposed to this: they consider this free use of *rakí* to be part of their cultural heritage.

WEBSITE FATIGUE

Cretan websites are often poorly maintained with little information. Rather than constantly updating their home pages, many local landlords have moved to social media sites. instead, with almost all events now only being posted there. Hoteliers would rather pay commissions of up to 20% to booking.com and airbnb. com than use professional agencies to create and maintain their URL. More and more private businesses have accounts on Facebook, Instagram and Linkedin, too. Just type in "*crete*" or "*kriti*" and wait for the seemingly endless loading of results.

LONG HAIR & A BEARD

Orthodox priests always wear their dark gowns, even if they are out shopping with their wife and children or are just enjoying a walk. They are allowed to marry, as celibacy is only required from the rank of bishop upwards. There are three other things which every *pappás* needs: a stiff hat, long hair and a proper beard. Hair loss appears to be rare – probably a sign of a healthy lifestyle. *Pappádes* can be seen frequently, even in bars, cafés and tavernas. Their job is secure even in a crisis because they are employed by the Greek state. There is no church tax in Hellas and no issue with people leaving the Church. Almost 98 per cent of Greeks belong to the Greek Orthodox Church.

SPARTANS ON THE SKIN

Tattoos are not only popular with the many British visitors to Crete. More and more Cretans are also having images permanently applied to their skin. As they don't weigh anything, they make popular souvenirs. How about a Greek letter on your back, or a carafe of *rakí* on your arm? Ghostly pirate ships, Spartan warriors, the philosopher Aristotle in front of the Acropolis in Athens and Greek sayings are currently among the hits at studios such as *Black Sheep* in Chaniá or *Dreamcatcher* in Kókkini Cháni.

NO NEED TO RUSH INTO ANYTHING

No one knows what tomorrow will bring. And the Cretans certainly don't. Nor do they make any long-term predictions. Which is why many major events and festivals – which northern Europeans usually start planning at least a year in advance – are only mentioned a few days before they take place. You'll often only find timetables and museum opening times on the Internet once they've been valid for a few days.

The Cretans even like to be a little vague when making personal arrangements. They'll arrange to meet in the morning or afternoon, evening or next week, and always add a *ta léme*: "We'll talk again". An hour before you're due to meet is still time enough to agree an exact time. Plus or minus half an hour, of course!

LOOK, THERE THEY ARE!

Vultures can be recognised by their tremendous wingspan as they circle in the sky. The roughly 300 griffon vultures on Crete have a wingspan of up to 2.60 m across, while the last ten (give or take) Cretan bearded cultures measure an impressive 3 m across. The best places to watch them gliding in the sky are the gorges to the west of the island. Crete's three types of eagle are even rarer than vultures: golden eagle, osprey and sea eagle. For excellent information on all these birds of prey go to *crete-birding.co.uk*.

BUILDING INSTEAD OF SAVING

Are the Greeks really so badly off? The numerous lovely houses and expensive cars would suggest otherwise. But things aren't as they seem: all the luxury goods were acquired before the crisis – although that doesn't mean they were all paid for. Banks were calling private individuals almost weekly to persuade them to take out loans. People who only wanted 20,000 euros found themselves with 50,000 euros. Spending instead of scrimping was the order of the day on the financial market. Now many Cretans are stuck with their debts. And the supposed securities on which the banks had been counting are no more. They don't even want to seize the goods. Because with such an abundance of high-debt houses, olive groves and fields, the individual debts are really not worth a lot.

A church in every village: testimony to the Cretans' strong Greek Orthodox beliefs

EATING
SHOPPING
SPORT

Réthimno: is the Cretans' love of vibrant colours inherited from the Venetians?

EATING & DRINKING

"If I want to eat alone, I can stay at home," says almost every Cretan. And before you know it, they have drummed up friends and relations and are headed for the taverna together. Which is why you'll usually only find tables for two in the places where the tourists go.

EATING IN COMPANY

This dining community which the Cretans call paréa means that no one orders just for themselves. Instead a variety of salads and delicious starters are ordered and everyone then helps themselves. Then the large platters of fish or grilled meat are also put on the table for everyone to share. Most Cretans do without dessert, because the portions are so generous and there are usually a lot of leftovers. It is not the done thing to finish the platters and plates completely, as this would suggest that the host hasn't been generous enough.

INSIDER TIP
Do not scrape your plate!

A LITTLE BIT OF EVERYTHING

As a tourist dining out alone or with a partner, you can of course order in the normal fashion – although the Cretan way is much more fun and you get to sample a variety of dishes. By the way: it is the Cretan custom that one person usually pays for everyone; if this does not suit you, then let the waiter know when you place your order. In the holiday resort areas, Cretans have adapted to the customs of the

Communal cooking and eating: Cretan style (left), and grilled vegetables on skewers (right)

holidaymakers by decorating the tavernas in the traditional way and bringing the food to the table hot. In recent years a number of restaurants have opened that serve haute cuisine. Their main clientele are the Cretans themselves and also Greek holidaymakers who value high-quality regional cuisine.

EXPENSIVE FISH

So, everyone finds what they are looking for: from inexpensive little snack bars serving *gyros* and *souvláki* to upmarket Italian restaurants with Mediterranean cuisine, and from simple family tavernas with home cooking to Cretan gourmet restaurants serving exquisite creations. No matter where you eat, if you order fresh fish, be prepared to pay high prices: you will not find anything under 40 euros per kilo.

BETTER & BETTER: CRETAN WINE

When dining out, Cretans drink water and beer or wine. A wide variety of Cretan wines are available, and the quality has improved substantially in recent years. Aside from wine by the glass and the affordable rétsina – Greek white wine infused with resin from the Aleppo pine – there are also a large number of quality wines from larger or smaller cellars. Wines from the cooperative wine cellars of Sitía and Péza near Iráklio are recommended. There are also some more exclusive wines available from independent cellars, such as *Lýrarákis*,

Typically Cretan: Greek coffee with water

Económou, Manoussákis, Michalákis and *Crétas Olympías. Boutáris* is a quality wine produced throughout Greece.

OPEN ALL HOURS

Most tavernas and restaurants are open from 9 am until well after midnight. Cretans seldom eat lunch before 1 pm and at night you will find them with their *paréa* dining at 10 pm or even later.

SWEET TREATS

Lovers of sweet delicacies can visit a *zacharoplastío,* the Greek version of a patisserie. Here you will find a wide variety of tarts, pastries, pralines and oriental pastries such as *baklavá* and *kataifi*, which look sweeter than they actually are, and the favourite *milópita* (apple pie) which is often served with vanilla ice cream.

COFFEE CULTURE

Cretan coffee houses are where the men meet. Every village has at least one *kafenío*, most have several *kafenía*. This is necessary because each *kafenío* is usually associated with one of the three main Greek political parties: the Conservatives, the Socialists or the Communists. Although operated by a private owner, the *kafenío* is something of a public institution. There is usually no obligation to order anything. The men sit down together to talk about God and the world and above all about Greek politics or to play *távli*, draughts or cards.

When you order a coffee for yourself, remember to say exactly how you prefer it. The Cretans drink Greek coffee, which is coffee brewed together with water and sugar. *Kafé ellinikó* is served in many variations: *skétto*, without sugar; *métrio*, with some sugar; *glikó*, with lots of sugar; *dipló*, a double shot. Instant coffee is also always available. Basically you order it as *neskafé* and specify the amount of sugar you prefer. There is also the option of *neskafé sestó*, hot Nescafé, or *frappé*, cold Nescafé whisked to a foam. Young Cretans love cold variants of coffee like *freddo espresso* and *freddo cappuccino*, and just like the Greek espresso, they are served with a glass of cold water.

Today's Specials

Starters

CHORIÁTIKI
A mixed Greek salad with goat's cheese and olives

FÁVA
Puréed yellow peas with onions and olive oil

KALITSÚNIA
Pastry filled with spinach or chard and fresh cheese

Main dishes

MOUSSAKÁ
A baked dish with minced meat, aubergines and béchamel sauce

PASTÍTSJO
Also a baked dish, made with macaroni, minced meat and béchamel sauce

STIFÁDO
Beef or rabbit stew with onions in a red sauce

JEMISTÉS
Tomatoes and peppers filled with rice, herbs and sometimes minced meat

Fish dishes

KAKAVIÁ
Fish soup similar to a bouillabaisse

SUPJÉS JEMISTÉS
Cuttlefish mainly filled with cheese

MARÍDES
Crispy fried small fish, eaten whole

KSIFÍA
Grilled boneless swordfish steak

Spirits

RAKÍ
Clear alcoholic pomace drink made from local grapes without any additives

OÚZO
Aniseed aperitif which becomes opaque when diluted with water

METAXÁ
The best-known Greek brandy

SHOPPING

In the souvenir shops in the cities and resorts you will find lots of mass-produced goods that are seldom made in Crete. It is better to shop in the alleyways of Chaniá and Réthimno, the shops in Ágios Nikólaos, the crafters' workshops on roadsides and in the villages.

THE TASTE OF CRETE

Olives, olive oil and honey are tasty and healthy souvenirs which can also be bought in Crete's numerous health food shops. Fruit preserves, dried fruit and several types of cheese are also typical of the island. A good selection of Cretan wines is available in specialist stores, called *cáva*. *Rakí* is sold everywhere, but ask for a tasting first because quality can vary a great deal.

MADE OF WOOD & CLAY

You will find modern and traditional ceramics all over Crete. Margarítes near Réthimno is a potters' village well worth visiting. Carvings from olive wood are particularly valuable because the wood has to be cured for a long time and is very difficult to work with. The largest selection can be found in Mátala on the southern coast. Not made of olive wood but great fun are the wooden, hand-painted bow ties and frames for sunglasses that you can buy in Iráklio.

HAND-CRAFTED JEWELLERY

In Crete you will still find some small gold and silversmiths who produce some of their wares themselves, e.g. in Chaniá's old town and the harbour at Ágios Nikólaos. Before you buy, always check the quality. It is probably best to decline the glass of ouzo offered by the sales assistants, but you can certainly rely on the hallmarks.

Great souvenirs include leather goods (left) and premium olive oil (right)

ANCIENT & MODERN

The museum shop in the Venetian log-gia in Réthimno offers the widest variety of replicas of ancient artefacts, and they also ship larger objects any-where in the world. A few jewellers opposite the Archaeological Museum in Iráklio also sell good (but unauthor-ised) copies of Minoan jewellery.

LEATHER ALLEY

Chaniá is the island's leather centre. Skrídloff is a long lane that sells masses of bags and accessories "Made in Greece" (or Italy). It's not necessarily the place to find *Georgína Skalídi*, whose luxurious bags are artistic one-offs, and available exclusively from her boutique in Chaniá.

IF THE SHOE FITS

When it comes to their footwear, the ladies of Crete really like to strut their stuff - whether that's in high heels, sandals or boots. Shoemakers Paiagnotákis of *Syrtós Handmade Shoes (Iráklio | Odós Sfakianáki 9)* take the (shoe) biscuit: they customise shoes to their clients' wishes – within 48 hours if required.

INSIDER TIP
Be nice to your feet

FASHION

Cretan fashionistas fly to Athens for their shopping; internationally renowned labels, plus popular brands such as Zara and H&M, can only be found in Iráklio town centre. High-quality T-shirts and children's clothing made in Crete are available from Ágios Nikólaos.

CRETAN SOUNDS

Whether it is traditional Cretan *lýra* sounds or the rock music of the Greek charts – you will find them in any music shop in Crete.

SPORT & ACTIVITIES

The mountains and sea are the island's sports arenas. Daredevils try their luck on Europe's second-highest bungee jump; the more cautious venture out for some yoga on an SUP board. Some like to attach themselves to a parachute and be pulled over the water, while cyclists can choose between mountain bikes, racing bikes and e-bikes.

BUNGEE JUMPING

A bungee jump at Arádena, near the south coast, takes bravery. You can dive 138 m from the bridge into the Arádena Gorge: *Liquidbungy (July–Aug Sat/Sun from noon | 100 euros | Arádena | mobile 69 37 61 51 91 | www.bungy.gr).* There is also the option of a more moderate drop from a crane by the sea at the *Star Beach Water Park* on the eastern edge of Chersónisos. The drop is only 50 m which also allows for tandem jumps:

Star Beach Bungee (daily from 10 am | approx. 60 euros | Chersónisos | www. starbeach.gr).

CLIMBING

The Asterússia Mountains on the south coast are an as-yet unknown El Dorado for climbers. Head for the village of *Kapetanianá*, where the contacts are Gunnar and Luisa Schuschnigg from Austria at *Korifi Tours (tel. 28 93 04 14 40 | www.korifi.de).* For comprehensive information on the various climbs there and elsewhere on Crete, contact *www.climbincrete.com.*

DANCING

Have you been infected by *Zorba the Greek*? Then get yourself over to the south coast and contact Swiss-born Isabella Müllenbach at the *Haus Kavoúri (tel. 69 76 01 17 33 | www. housekavouri.com).* She gives weekly lessons in Greek dancing in Soúda at

Hiking through the Samariá Gorge is not for the faint-hearted

Plakiás, and you can also join in a few sessions on the spur of the moment.

DIVING

Cretan diving sites are particularly suited to beginners due to their crystal-clear water, good centres and interesting underwater rock formations. However, there are few fish to be seen. In Crete archaeologists also have a say in the approval of dive sites as they fear that divers will disturb excavations and even smuggle pieces out of the country.

A few diving schools (some also offer introductory courses for adults and for children): ⚓ *Atlantis Diving Centre (Beach Hotel | Ádele)* and in the *Club Marine Palace Hotel (Panórmo | tel. 28 31 07 16 40 | www.atlantis-creta.com); Creta Maris Dive Center (Liménas Chersónisou | Hotel Creta Maris |tel. 28 97 02 21 22| www.dive-cretamaris.gr); Dive Together (on* *the coastal road | Plakiás | tel. 28 32 03 23 13 | www.dive2gether. com); Notos Mare (at the new harbour | Chóra Sfakíon tel. 28 25 09 13 33 | www.notosmare. com).*

HIKING

The E4 European long-distance hiking trail stretches from the west to the east coast of Crete. You should allow at least four weeks for the complete hike. The signposting is good but not perfect. Fitness is essential because you will be crossing mountains, and a tent is also useful *(www.oreivatein.com)*. Particularly popular and easy to manage on holiday by experienced mountain hikers are the four sections of the route between Paleochóra and Chóra Sfakíon, totalling approx. 60 km. If you lose interest mid-way, you can board the coastal steamer to continue your journey.

You can also undertake many hikes on Crete on your own or book one- or two-week hikes through specialist travel agencies at home or in Crete, such as *Happy Walker (Odós Tombázi 56 | Réthimno | tel. 28 31 03 13 90 | www.happywalker.com)*.

HORSE RIDING

Riding stables for experienced riders are at the *Horsefarm Melanoúri* in Pitsídia *(tel. 28 92 04 50 40)* and the *Odysseia Stables (tel. 28 97 05 10 80, mobile 69 42 83 60 83 | www. horseriding.gr)* in Avdoú en route to the Lassíthi Plateau. Both offer accommodation as well. Guided hacks for absolute beginners are available from stables in and around *Liménas Chersónisou*.

MOUNTAIN BIKING

Crete is an ideal destination for mountain bikers. There are lots of good biking centres that offer a range of tour packages for all levels of difficulty. Those who prefer to take it easy can take a support van up to the starting point and then cycle downhill, while ambitious bikers can challenge themselves cycling between mountain peaks. Organisers offer day trips *(approx. 40–60 euros, children 25–40 euros)* and week packages. E-bikes are generally available too.

Good agencies are *Adventurebikes (on the road from the town square to the beach | tel. 69 37 90 42 51 | adventurebikes.org)* in Georgioúpoli; *Freak Mountainbike Centre (mobile 69 85 81 02 40 | www.freak-mountainbike.com)* in Palékastro; *Hellas Bike*

(main road opposite the Bank of Cyprus | tel. 28 21 06 08 58 | www. hellasbike.net) in Agía Marína near Chaniá; *Olympic Bike (Adelianós Kámbos 32 | tel. 28 31 07 27 83 | www.olympicbike.com)* on the coastal road east of Réthimno; and *Anso Travel (tel. 28 32 03 17 12 | www. ansovillas.com)* in Plakiás on the south coast. There are five centres affiliated to *Crete Cycling (tel. on Crete 69 86 92 77 06 | www.crete-cycling. com)* in Ágios Nikólaos, Móchlos, Palékastro and Iráklio (all year), and Agía Galíni (which also has racing bikes). A good bike costs 13–22 euros a day or 80–115 euros per week. Challenging day trips on e-mountain bikes in very small groups are arranged by Adam Frogákis *(tel. 69 44 74 06 93 | www.adams-ebikes-crete.com)*. After being collected from the hotel between Iráklio and Sisi, it's off to the multilingual guide's home for an extensive breakfast.

RUNNING

Marathons are held on Crete several times a year. These events also allow runners to cover shorter distances such as 5 or 10 km. In June, a 35-km race starts on the Nída mountain plateau and leads up to the peak of Mount Psilorítis.

SAILING

With an experienced skipper from *Pélagos Dive Centre (tel. 28 41 02 43 76 | divecrete.com/English/Sailing.html)* on board you

Riding on the beach near Liménas Chersónisou

can go sailing on a private yacht from Ágios Nikólaos to the islands of Spinalónga or Móchlos. From Ierápetra you can sail to the island of Chrisí with *Nautilos (Odós Markopoúlou 1 | mobile 69 72 89 42 79 | www. nautiloscruises.gr)*. You are welcome to lend a hand but it is not necessary.

WATER SPORTS

Almost all the popular beaches offer water sports options, from water skiing to jet skiing and parasailing. Paddle boats and canoes can also be hired in front of the larger hotels and surfboards are available on many of the beaches, mainly on the north and east coast. Good windsurfing schools can be found at the larger centres such as *Freak Station (tel. 69 79 25 38 61 | www.freak-surf.com)* on *Koureménos Beach* in Palékastro, who also specialise in kite surfing.

The specialist in stand-up paddling (SUP) is the Cretan *Stéfanos Averkiou (Station Akrotíri peninsula, Loutráki, on the beach by the Mare Nostrum Villas | tel. 69 45 50 09 39 | www. supincrete.com)* from Chaniá. His offer includes hire, courses and guided day trips, and yoga on a paddleboard is his speciality.

REGIONAL OVERVIEW

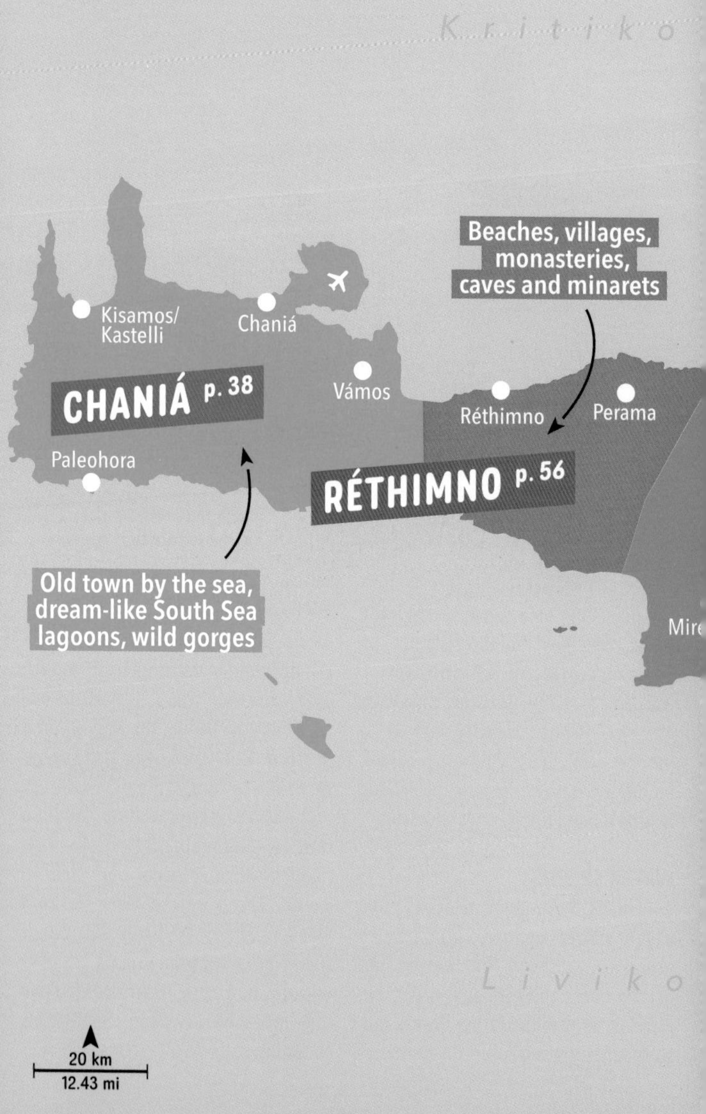

Kritiko

Kisamos/
Kastelli

Chaniá

✈

Beaches, villages, monasteries, caves and minarets

CHANIÁ p. 38

Vámos

Réthimno

Perama

RÉTHIMNO p. 56

Paleohora

Old town by the sea, dream-like South Sea lagoons, wild gorges

Mire

Liviko

▲
20 km
12.43 mi

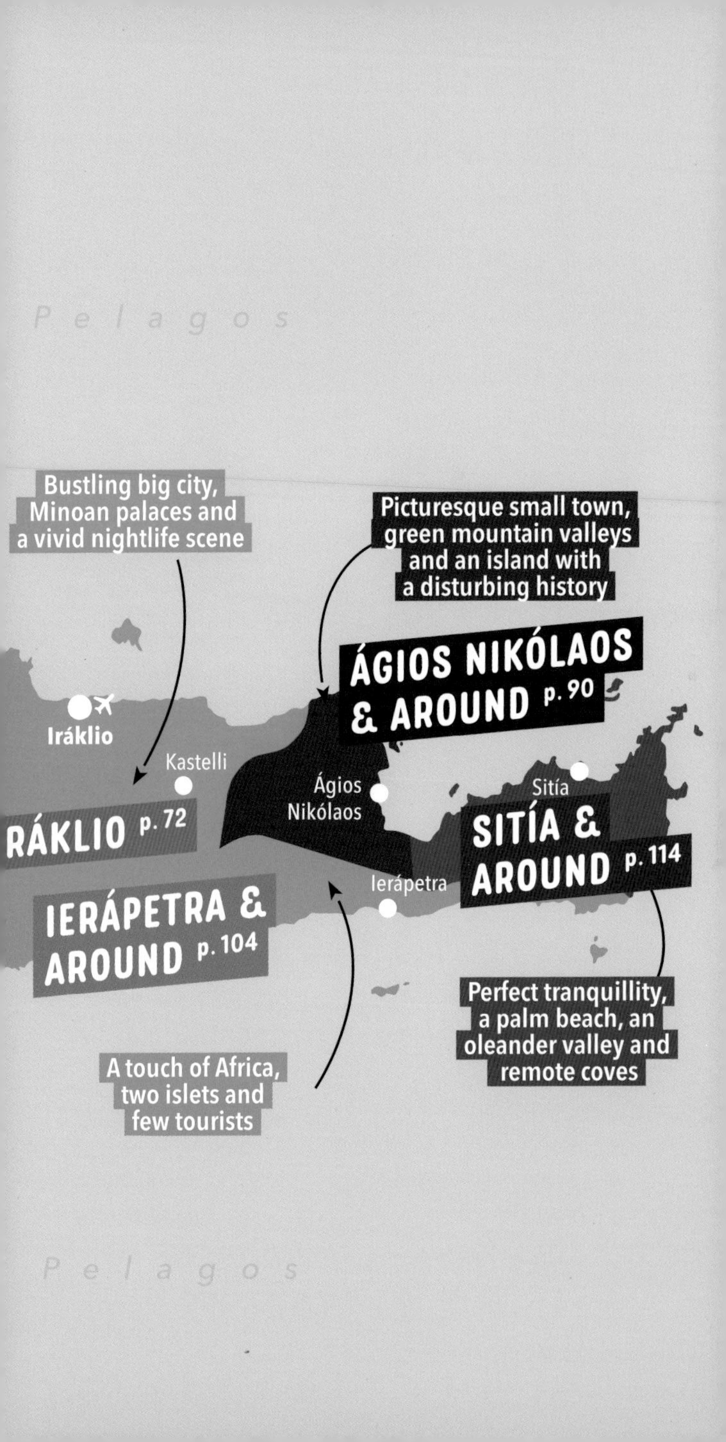

Pelagos

Bustling big city,
Minoan palaces and
a vivid nightlife scene

Picturesque small town,
green mountain valleys
and an island with
a disturbing history

ÁGIOS NIKÓLAOS
& AROUND p. 90

✈
Iráklio

Kastelli

Ágios
Nikólaos

Sitía

SITÍA &
AROUND p. 114

RÁKLIO p. 72

IERÁPETRA &
AROUND p. 104

Ierápetra

Perfect tranquillity,
a palm beach, an
oleander valley and
remote coves

A touch of Africa,
two islets and
few tourists

Pelagos

CHANIÁ

CRETE'S WILD WEST

Born to be wild? Then Chaniá in western Crete is the perfect holiday region for you. The White Mountains contain almost more gorges than villages, while between the rough cliff faces of the Libyan Sea are isolated beaches and only a few tiny villages.

Some of these villages can only be reached by boat. In the lagoons in the extreme west, you'll swim in turquoise waters reminiscent of the South Seas, while in the protected valleys you can pick oranges straight from the trees. Sheep graze between ancient ruins, while the

A perfect catwalk – Chaniá's harbour promenade

Middle Ages surround you in the old town of Chaniá. You won't find many of the bathing resorts in this part of the island advertised in holiday brochures – these ones are mostly for independent travellers.

Chaniá (pop. 108,000) is the main city in the region and the most beautiful of Crete's towns. Boredom is unheard of in the island's second-largest town. Hotels and guesthouses often have a roof garden, from where you can see the vast Aegean and the almost 2,500-m-high mountain peaks.

CHANIÁ

Kritikó Pélagos

Rodopoú

8 Bálos Beach ★

Gramvoúsa

Ροδωπός
Rodopós

Κολυμβάρι
Kolimbari

Μάλεμε
Máleme

Καλυδονία
Kalydonia

Καλυβιανή
Kaliviani

Βούβες
Vouves

Ζουνάκι
Zounaki

Πλαταν
Platan

Φαλάσαρνα
Falasarna

Δραπανιάς
Drapanias

Kissámos **7**

Κουφε
Kouf

Πλάτανος
Platanos

Ποταμίδα
Potamida

6 Polirrinía

Βατόλακκ
Vatolakko

Λουσακιές
Lousakies

Τοπόλια
Topolia

Σφηνάρι
Sfinari

Μελίσσια
Melissia

Σηρικάρι
Sirikari

47 km, 70 mins

Πλαγιά
Plaghia

Κεφαλή
Kefali

Βλάτος
Vlatos

Μυλωνες
Milones

Πρασές
Prases

Αμυγδαλοκεφάλι
Amigdalokefali

Έλος
Elos

Χρυσοσκαλίτισσα
Chrisoskalitissa

Πλεμενιανά
Plemeniana

11 Iríni-Schlucht

Επανωχώρι
Epanochori

Καλλιθέα
Kallithea

9 Elafonísi Beach ★

Λαγκαδάς
Lagkadas

Ροδοβάνι
Rodováni

Μονή
Moni

Άνυδροι
Anydri

12 Soúgia

10 Paleochóra

▲
6 km
3.73 mi

Livikó Pélago

Σταυρός
Stavros

Καμπάνι
Kampani

α Μαρίνα
a Marína

Harbour ★

① Akrotíri Peninsula ★

● **Chaniá**
p. 42

Old Town ★

Καθιανά
Kathiana

Στέρνες
Sternes

ατάς
latas

Όαση
Oasi

Σούδα
Souda

Νερόκουρος
Nerokouros

Κόκκινο Χωριό
Kokkino Chorio

② Áptera

Καλύβες
Kalyves

Παπαδολιανά
Papadoliana

Νέο Χωριό
Neo Chorio

Δράπανος
Drapanos

⑤ Fournés
νές
es

Ραμνή
Ramni

Δρακόνα
Drakona

Vámos ③

Κεφαλάς
Kefalas

Μεσκλά
Meskla

Νίπος
Nipos

Βρύσες
Vrises

Μελιδόνι
Melidoni

Βαφές
Vafes

④ Georgioúpoli

42 km, 4 hrs

Αλίκαμπος
Alikambos

Δράμια
Dramia

ΡΗΤΕ
ΚΡΗΤΗ

Αμουδάρι
Amoudari

Ίμβρος
Imbros

⑬ Ímbros-Schlucht

ουμέλη
Roumeli

Άγιος Ιωάννης
Agios Ioannis

Ανώπολη
Anopoli

Πατσιανός
Patsianos

⑭ Loutró

⑮ Chóra Sfakíon

20 km, 60 mins

Órthi-Ámmos Beach

⑯ Frangokastéllo

CHANIÁ TOWN

(🗺 D–E2) **The regional capital, Chaniá, is worth a few days of your holiday; of all the Cretan towns, it is the beauty queen. And it has a lot to offer to visitors.**

A good programme would start with museums and plenty of maritime touches in the morning; enjoy lunch in the harbour and some downtime in the hammam. Then do some relaxed, exclusive shopping, followed by dinner in the old Turkish baths and a carriage ride. The evening can continue with some traditional lyre music and, later on, jazz until sunrise. You won't have to leave the ★ *old town*, which was shaped by the Venetians.

The new town has nothing to offer apart from the entertaining City Park.

SIGHTSEEING

HARBOUR ★

A blessing in disguise: because the harbour in Chaniá is so silted up, the only boats that can enter are fishing boats and yachts. This means that the long harbour quay is almost traffic-free, which makes it perfect for a stroll. The only vehicles on the tarmac are horse-drawn carriages. Cafés and tavernas nestle cheek by jowl between the *Maritime Museum* and the eye-catching but ugly *Janissaries Mosque*. After that, the quayside gets quieter as you pass more or less preserved Venetian shipyards and a few basic fish restaurants before reaching the *Minoan ship* and the nighttime

Minoan masterpieces: painted sarcophagi in the Archaeological Museum

party quarter on the east side of the harbour. A long jetty stretches west of here on which you can walk or jog.

MARITIME MUSEUM

How lovely that models exist. This shipping museum shows us what the town looked like in the year 1600. History lovers in particular will appreciate the retelling of the historic sea battles with miniature ships; you can even have a close look at a Venetian galley ship. On the top floor, Germans and Austrians are confronted by a dark chapter in their history: the attack on Crete in 1941. *Mon-Sat 9 am-5 pm, Sun 10 am-6 pm, in winter daily 9 am-3.30 pm | admission 3 euros | Aktí Kundurióti | mar-mus-crete.gr |* ○ *30-45 mins*

TOPANÁS

Oh, sweet seduction! You'll struggle to resist the plethora of tiny shops and artists' studios that have opened up in the old district of Topanás.

Quality and originality abound on straight-as-a-die Odós Theotokópoulou and its side streets, and if you climb

up the *Schiávo bastion* you'll be able to see over the old town to the sea.

JEWISH QUARTER

Narrow streets, tiny shops, cosy tavernas: the Odós Kondiláki is worth a visit. The town's Jewish community lived here until the Holocaust. All that remains of it is the tiny *Etz Hayyim synagogue (May-Oct Mon-Thu 10 am-6 pm, Fri 10 am-3 pm, Nov-April Mon-Thu 10 am-5 pm, Fri 10 am-3 pm)*, which was a Christian church until 1669. International voluntary guides are available to take you around (for a donation of 2 euros) and will tell you about what happens in a synagogue.

ARCHAEOLOGICAL MUSEUM

Crete's loveliest museum is a Gothic church from Venetian times. The most interesting things about it are the primitive hunting scenes on sarcophagi that are over 3,300 years old. A tiny seal from the 15th century BCE is unique, and can also be seen on the museum's (free) brochure. It is of a monumental lance-bearer on the rooftops of Minoan Chaniá. *April-Oct daily 8 am-8 pm, Nov-March Tue-Sun 8 am-3 pm | admission 4 euros | Odós Chalidón 25 |* ○ *30-40 mins*

FOLKLORE MUSEUM

If you think museums are dead, then try this one. You'll see craftsmen sitting in their historic workshops, while a vintner distills *rakí* all year round, and a grandmother shivers by the fire even in summer. The fact that they are all made of wax has the advantage that your photos will be nice and clear. *Mon, Tue, Thu, Fri 9 am–6 pm, Wed, Sat 9 am–5 pm, Sun 11 am–4 pm | admission 3 euros | Odós Chalidón 46b | ⏱ 30–40 mins*

ÁGIOS NIKÓLAOS CHURCH

You won't see this anywhere else: a church with a minaret! When the Turks conquered Crete in 1669, they converted many of the Christian churches into Islamic places of prayer. All they had to do was remove the icons, paint over or scrape off the murals, install a prayer recess facing Mecca, and place a minaret on top. After 1913, these mosques were turned back into churches. All the other minarets were removed, but this one was eventually restored. *Platía 1821*

MINOAN SHIP

Would you row from Crete to Piraeus? A Cretan team attempted it in 2004 and, despite the auxiliary sails, it took them 27 days to sail the 390 km. What made it even more amazing: the bold men and women were travelling in the same kind of boat as the Minoans would have used for their long-distance sailing expeditions over 3,300 years before. Today, this scientifically based reproduction is housed in an old Venetian shipyard, where video films tell you more about the construction and trip of the *Minoa*. *May–Oct Mon–Sat 9 am–5 pm, Sun 10 am–6 pm | admission 2 euros | Odós Defkalónia | ⏱ 15–20 mins*

CITY PARK 👫

Few tourists visit Chaniá's "green lung". Local Chanioti sit in the chicest, most traditional coffee house on the island, *O Kípos (daily from 8 am | €€)*, playing cards, Távli, Scrabble and Monopoly as they drink their *cafés ellinikós* or a glass of champagne. A few steps further on, Cretan wild goats with their mighty horns graze quietly, while in the evenings, films are shown in the summer cinema under the starry sky. *Odós Dimokratías/Odós Tzanakáki*

Food, drink, strolling and watching the world go by: an evening by the harbour

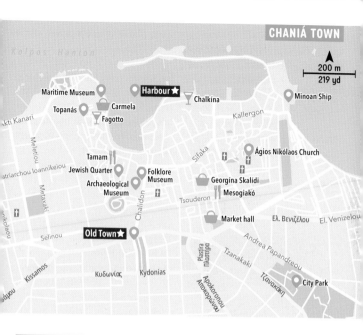

CHANIÁ TOWN

200 m
219 yd

Kolpos Hanion

Maritime Museum
Topanás
Carmela
Fagotto
Harbour ★
Chalkína
Minoan Ship
Kallergon
Sifaka
Tamam
Jewish Quarter
Archaeological Museum
Folklore Museum
Ágios Nikólaos Church
Georgína Skalídi
Mesogiakó
Chalidon
Tsouderon
Market hall
Old Town ★
Selinou
Ελ. Βενιζέλου
El. Venizelo
Andrea Papandreou
Plastira Πλαστηρα
Tzanakaki
Kυδωνίας Kydonias
City Park

EATING & DRINKING

MESOGIAKÓ

In his small, modernly furnished tavern in the old part of the city, restaurateur Michális Pedinákis offers Mediterranean dishes including lamb served without the usual bones. The wide choice of salads is particularly tasty. Homemade panna cotta is the perfect dessert. *Daily from noon | Odós Chatzimicháli Daligiánni 36 | mesogiako.com | €€*

TAMAM

This taverna in what was once a Turkish bath is a meeting place for local intellectuals and artists. The food is a combination of recipes from the two important Greek cities that are now in Turkey, Smýrna (now Izmir) and Constantinople (now Istanbul). *Daily from noon | Odós Zambéliu 49 | tamamrestaurant.com | €€*

SHOPPING

CARMELA

In this tiny shop run by Carmela and Dimitri Iatrópoulou you'll have all the time in the world to look around in peace. No single item of jewellery or pottery is repeated, and everything was made either by the owners themselves or by their Greek friends. Allow Carmela to recommend the right gemstone to match your skin tone and bank balance. *Odós Angélu 7*

INSIDER TIP
Kitsch-free zone

GEORGÍNA SKALÍDI

Do you find symmetry boring? Post-modern clutch-bags are this designer's passion, and she designs them all herself in coloured leather. A recent addition to her range includes brilliant costume jewellery, which is surprisingly affordable. *Mon–Sat 11 am–2 pm, Tue, Thu, Fri also 6–9 pm | Odós Chatzimicháli Dalagiánni 58 | georginaskalidi.com*

INSIDER TIP
Out of the ordinary

MUNICIPAL MARKET

This century-old building now also has souvenir sellers mixed in with the greengrocers and fishmongers. The most traditional and original aspect of the market are its quaint 🍴 tavernas. *Mon, Wed, Sat 8.30 am–5 pm, Tue, Thu, Fri 8.30 am–9.30 pm | Platía Venizélos*

SPORT & ACTIVITIES

There are always some drivers with their one-horse carriages waiting for customers by the harbour. Tours around the old town last 20 or 50 minutes and cost 15 or 45 euros respectively. The best times are at dusk and in the early evening, with departures from the Mosque of the Janissaries/Yali Mosque. For a more active exploration of Chaniá during the day or at night , rent a *segway (39–60 euros / 75–120 mins | Odós Ep. Chrisánthou 25 | tel. 69 44 59 71 59 | chaniasegwaytours. com).* Regular bus services to the big 🚲 *Aqua Creta Limnoúpolis* fun water

park *(limnoupolis.gr)* depart from Platía 1866.

BEACHES

The beach to the west of the old town may suffice for a quick dip, but for a long day's swimming you'd do better to take a public bus to Stavrós (*E2*) on the Akrotíri peninsula, to Almirída and Kalíves (*F3*) or to Plataniás (*D2*).

WELLNESS

AL HAMAM

The most original and also the smallest of all wellness oases on the island is at Chaniá harbour. It has an old-world atmosphere, but is actually high-tech. Step onto the roof and drink your Turkish tea from one of the typical small glasses. You will almost feel as if you are in a sultan's palace. *Mon–Fri 11 am–10 pm, Sat/Sun noon–10 pm | from 25 euros / 45 mins | Pl. El. Venizélou 14 | tel. 28 21 05 90 05 | alhammam.gr*

INSIDER TIP
Oriental flavours

NIGHTLIFE

There's plenty going on in the old town all year round. The standard discos, beloved of the happy-drinker tourists, are just behind the Janissaries Mosque in the harbour on the short Odós Sourméli. The *Klik Bar* is always popular. The local in-crowd prefers to meet in the music clubs on the eastern side of the harbour, behind the striking Hotel Porto Veneziano. For those with slightly different tastes in music, there's a jazz club and numerous tavernas with Cretan lyre performances.

CHALKÍNA

Greek and Cretan live music is played daily at this modern *ouzerí* on the harbour, at weekends in winter from 10 pm. Mainly locals gather here. *Aktí*

Tombázi 29–30 | chalkina.com

FAGOTTO

If you'd rather leave the rocking to others and prefer instead to enjoy good, solid jazz and rock in a cosy bar or down a narrow street in the old town, then the relaxed, well-established Fagotto is your musical home from home. *Daily 9 pm–5 am | Odós Ángelou 16*

An increasing number of souvenir sellers have now joined the food vendors in the market

In Áptera you can have a great picnic between antique relics and the remains of a monastery

AROUND CHANIÁ

🚩 AKROTÍRI PENINSULA ★

50–60 km round trip / approx. 3 hrs from Chaniá by car, 5½ hrs incl. hike
You'll be caught between monasteries and military cannons here: tax-payers' money goes up in smoke at NATO's rocket-launch site on the peninsula, while the monks in two monasteries pray for peace. And although you can only see the military barracks from a distance, you are welcome to visit the monasteries. The monks at *Agía Triáda (daily from 9 am–6 pm | admission 2 euros)* work busily producing olive oil, wine and schnapps. You can also visit the wine cellar with the adjoining tasting room and the 17th-century church with its traditional murals.

Prayer and the lovely garden are the main interests of the extremely devout monks at the 16th-century *Gouvernéto Monastery (Sun 5–11 am and 5–8 pm, Oct–Easter 4–7 pm; Mon, Tue, Thu, Sat 10 am–1 pm and 5–6 pm | admission free)*, which strongly resembles a desert fort. Modest clothing is essential here. Fancy a little walk? There is a proper path from the Gouvernéto Monastery through the quiet landscape past a chapel in a stalactite cave to the now-abandoned *Katholikó Monastery* beside a gorge. *▥ E–F2*

🅱 ÁPTERA

16 km / 25 mins from Chaniá by car
Romantic ruins will draw you to the

rocky plateau near the coast. In spring, you'll share the tiers of the ancient theatre with scarlet poppies. The backdrop of the White Mountains against green valleys also merits a round of applause. Check out your echo in one of the two vast Roman cisterns, then unpack your picnic in the courtyard of a medieval abbey. The attendant limits his activities to selling tickets at the ticket desk, so you're free to explore as you wish *(Tue–Sun 8 am–3 pm | admission 3 euros)*.

As you continue on the short drive to the Ottoman fort on the escarpment of the plateau, you'll come across the remains of the once miles-long town wall and will pass fields of giant fennel, which the earlier

fishermen and sailors used as fire lighters. Break open one of the dried stalks (which grow to lengths of up to 2 m) in late summer or autumn, and you can make the pulp in them glow. Just hold a cigarette lighter or match to it, blow for a few seconds, and you'll have a glimmer. And that is exactly how Prometheus first brought fire to mankind on earth. *E3*

❸ VÁMOS

22 km / 40 mins from Chaniá by car
If gentle tourism is just your thing, you should rent a village house in Vámos (pop. 700) through *Vamos Traditional Village (tel. 28 25 02 21 90 | vamos-village.gr | €€–€€€)*. You'll quickly become part of the community and find yourself sitting among the locals on the (not yet traffic-free) *platía*. By

the time of your second visit you will be greeted like a close friend. In 1995, a group of young people in the large main town on the Apokóronas peninsula had the idea of restoring empty old houses and renting them out. Above an old cistern on the main street is the taverna *Stérna tou Bloumósifis (daily from 11 am | €€)*, which serves creative Cretan cuisine.

The group also owns the travel agency on Vámos's old main street, which, as well as providing accommodation, also arranges guided hikes, cooking courses and agricultural activities, visits to wineries and cheese dairies. However, you'll need a car, because it's 7 km to the next beach, the *Almirída Beach*. The only buses to the beach and Chaniá go early in the morning and at lunchtime. *F3*

4 GEORGIOÚPOLI

40 km / 40 mins from Chaniá by car
The mix is right: Georgioúpoli is a typical Cretan village with a perfectly good life of its own, and yet it is perfectly prepared for holidaymakers as well. Fishermen still bring their catches to the river harbour in the mornings, and then head over to the *kafenió*. Pedalos and kayaks are for hire right under the bridge; you can take them up the river and watch the turtles. Grannies, grandpas and nursing mums settle down on the modern *platía* to watch the tourists.

A 14-km sandy beach starts just to the east of the harbour, and there's still plenty of space between the hotels there. Public buses go to nearby Réthimno and to Chaniá at least every

hour, while there are lots of quiet villages in the surrounding area that offer pure rusticity.

🚂 *Fun trains* take tourists into the surrounding countryside and even to the nearby *Lake Kournás*, which is just 3km away. It is the largest mountain lake on the island, and offers a beach, tavernas and pedal-boat hire. Mountain bikes are available to hire from *Adventurebikes* (see p. 34) on the street from the *platía* to the beach. They also offer guided quad tours off road. At night, *Café Titos* on the *platía* and the *Beach Bar Tropicana* become clubs. *F3–4*

5 FOURNÉS

15 km / 25 mins from Chaniá by car
Could it be any healthier! The *Taverne* of the 50-acre *Botanical Park of Crete (March–mid-Nov daily from 9 am until 75 mins before sunset | admission 6 euros | on the road to Ómalos | botanical-park.com | €€)* serves only freshly squeezed juices from fruit they harvested themselves. And you can rest assured we're not just talking about the oranges that grow on tens of thousands of trees here in Fournés and the surrounding villages, but also about more exotic varieties such as papaya, guava, passionfruit and kiwi.

The kitchen prepares typical Cretan dishes flavoured with local herbs, lime and lemongrass, and bakes its own bread in the wood-fired oven.

Not hungry? Then go for a walk along the 3 km of trails through the Mediterranean and tropical gardens, and we'll talk again. *D3*

Kíssamos is the starting point for excursions to the fortified island of Gramvoúsa

⑥ POLIRRINÍA

53 km / 75 mins from Chaniá by car

Alone at last! It's unusual to see strangers in this tiny mountain village, which 2,500 years ago was an important town. Your best choice is to follow the small signpost to the Acropolis. At the point where the road ends between the walls of the old houses is the medieval church *Ágii Patéres*, with lots of old inscriptions on its exterior walls. They were originally part of a temple, and you can still see the stone blocks used for the supporting walls on the edge of the churchyard, as well as an old circular threshing floor. A 15-minute walk along the narrow footpath will take you through the maquis and up a rocky hill with all sorts of antique walls along the slopes. The tiny chapel is the perfect place for a picnic in complete isolation.

INSIDER TIP
Heavenly shade

To get back to the village, follow the sign with "O Vráchos" on it, and *Giórgos Tsichlákis* will be waiting for you. The former carpenter sells lovely items made of wood in his studio, including highly imaginative wind chimes. Every October he distills his own *rakí*, which he flavours with a selection of his home-grown herbs. You are welcome to sit on his terrace and sample it, if you like. When you then stroll through the village, you will see other ancient and medieval walls, including the remains of a water system and a cistern from the time of the Roman Emperor Hadrian. *B3*

⑦ KISSÁMOS

42 km / 40 mins from Chaniá by car

Far from the mainstream, you're now in Crete's westernmost little town in the sun. For most visitors to Crete, Kíssamos (pop. 3,000) is only the starting point for the boat trip to *Bálos Beach* (see p. 52). The only tourist attraction as such is the approximately 150-m-long beach promenade with cafés and tavernas including the *Kelári (€€)*. West of that is a good sandy beach, while to the east is a 1-km-long shingle beach. Opposite the *Archaeological Museum (Tue–Sun 8 am–3 pm | admission 2 euros | Platía Tzanakáki)*, with its lovely mosaic floors, is the *Strata Tours (Platia Tzanakáki | tel. 28 22 02 42 49 | stratatours.com)* travel agency, which hires out bicycles. Owner Stélios goes hiking with visitors, and will even take you into some of the houses in the villages. ▢ B2

8 BÁLOS BEACH ★ ⚘
52 km / 75 mins from Chaniá by car (to the car park) or 80 mins from Kissámos by boat

Wow! Whether you come on the excursion boat from Kissámos or on foot from the car park at the end of a rough track, the views of the lagoon of *Bálos* with its white beaches against the bare cliffs will bowl you over. And apart from a single taverna, there are no buildings in sight; not even campers are allowed to stay overnight here. Sailors can also explore the island of *Gramvoúsa* with its Venetian fort on the way over. Car drivers and hikers can ride a donkey down from the car park to the beach. Travel here along a 7-km track that is suitable (with care!) for cars *(toll 2 euros)* from the village of Kaliviani. Boat trips from Kissámos are offered by *Cretan Daily Cruises (daily approx. 9.30 am | 25 euros | tel.*

28 22 02 43 44 | *cretandailycruises. com)*. ▢ A2

9 ELAFONÍSI BEACH ★ ⚘
78 km / 2 hrs from Chaniá by car

Blue, turquoise or green? The still waters on the finest sand shimmer on this beach in every imaginable hue. This has made the beach extremely popular with visitors, especially in high summer. Tavernas and guesthouses have been banished to the hinterland, and water sports are banned. So nature comes into its own. Those who would like to have Elafonísi mostly to themselves should stay here or in the neighbouring village of Chrissoskalítissa, where the eponymous, blindingly white monastery can also be seen in a highly photogenic position on a rock. ▢ A4

10 PALEOCHÓRA
77 km / 100 mins from Chaniá by car

It doesn't get any warmer than this! The large village on the south coast is the warmest place in the whole of Greece. Farmers take advantage of this for the countless solar-heated greenhouses all over the coastal plain. And tourists like it because they can sit outside all night even in spring and autumn. The community and hosts are happy to play along. Every day at 7 pm, the main street turns into a long *Food Court*, with tavernas, cafés and bars. Just a few steps, and you'll be in the garden of the island's first wine bar, *Monika's Garden (daily from 6 pm | on the road from the main junction to the sandy beach | €€)*, or you can

Looking even more beautiful from a distance: the lagoon of Bálos

watch classic films and the latest blockbusters at the *Summer Cinema*.

There is a long, extra-wide sandy beach on one side of the peninsula with the village. The other side will be for people who prefer to lie on shingle. All sorts of boat trips start in the tiny harbour, while quiet mountain villages in the region are good destinations for hikers. The only historical sight in the village is the freely accessible Venetian castle complex *Kástro Sélino,* which has one main purpose: people meet here at sunset. Night owls usually experience the sunrise at *Ágios Bar* on the main junction in the village. There's plenty of time to go to bed after that. *□□ B5*

⑪ IRÍNI GORGE

56 km / 70 mins from Chaniá by car
The Iríni Gorge is just as impressive as the Samariá Gorge but not as well known. The rock faces soar hundreds

of metres high; many parts of the gorge are covered in forest and huge boulders lie in the summer-dry river bed. The hike starts at the southern edge of the village of *Agía Iríni* on the road from Chaniá to Soúgia. A small forest restaurant is at the entrance. The gorge ends after 7 km at the simple little *Taverna Oásis (€),* which fits in perfectly with the landscape. The selection is limited but the food is authentic. Here you are also welcome to eat your picnic, provided that you order the drinks, such as hot mountain tea. From here a road continues for 5 km to Soúgia *(taxi booking tel. 28 23 05 14 84 or tel. 28 23 05 14 85). □□ C4*

INSIDER TIP
Bring your own food

⑫ SOÚGIA

70 km / 100 mins from Chaniá by car
There isn't much to say about Soúgia,

Plenty of sea and peacefulness for dinner in quiet, pedestrianised Loutró

which is precisely why regulars keep returning there every year. There are no other towns or villages as far as the eye can see; nothing worth visiting, no "you've-simply-got-to-see-this" pressures. With a crystal-clear conscience, you can focus entirely on enjoying the long shingle beach, the mix of Cretan and Alsatian cuisine served at the *Ómikron (€€)*, meet other Soúgia fans at the *Lotos Music Café* next door, and perhaps agree to share a sea taxi with them to a nearby beach. *C4*

⒔ ÍMBROS GORGE

57 km / 70 mins from Chaniá by car

Glutton for punishment or slacker? If you think hiking through the world-famous Samariá Gorge (see p. 138) is a little too strenuous, or you have become addicted to gorges, or if you're simply visiting Crete too early or too late in the year, then this easy-to-hike alternative is the solution for you. The Ímbros Gorge is almost as beautiful as its famous sister, but shorter, shallower and not so full of people. It starts in the village of *Ímbros* on the southern edge of the Askífou high plain, and ends about three hours later in Komitádes. The hosts of the tavernas will organise your transfer to the bus stop in *Chóra Sfakíon* (see p. 55) or back to your car in Ímbros for you. *Open during day-time | admission 2 euros | F4*

⒕ LOUTRÓ

73 km / 100 mins from Chaniá to Chóra Sfakíon by car, then by boat taxi

Do you yearn for a traffic-free world? Well, your dream can come true in Loutró. The only way to get to this blue-and-white town on the south coast is by boat or on foot; there are no cars. But it does have several tavernas right on the water's edge and no noise at all. You swim from the rocks and in tiny bays. A 30-minute walk will take you to the completely undeveloped shingle beach of Glikánera, where fresh and salt water mix. *E5*

15 CHÓRA SFAKÍON

73 km / 100 mins from Chaniá by car

Do you love bends? Then you'll travel through paradise when you come here from the northern coast: 20 tight hairpin bends take you from the Askífou high plain down to the Libyan Sea and tiny Chóra Sfakíon, which despite having a population of only 265 is nonetheless able to proud to call itself the capital of the Sfakiá. From here there are ferries along the southern coast to *Paleochóra* (see p. 52) that also stop in *Agía Rouméli*, the destination of any hike through the *Samariá Gorge* (see p. 138). Car ferries chug across to *Gávdos*, Europe's southernmost island, where you can spend a night under the starry skies. Or a sea taxi will take you to the completely traffic-free bathing resort of *Loutró* (see p. 54), which also has a tiny beach right on the outskirts. So if you'd like to do a lot of hiking and spend time on the water, this is the perfect place for you for a few days. *E5*

16 FRANGOKASTÉLLO

80 km / 2 hrs from Chaniá by car

If you're scared of ghosts, then stay away from this Venetian *castle (daily from 9 am–5 pm | admission 2 euros)* on 17 May, as that is when it is visited by the spirits of the Cretan freedom fighters who in 1828 tried to occupy the castle but were besieged by the Turks and massacred. You can safely enter on any other day of the year. Right outside is a wide, extremely flat sandy beach. Around 400 m further east you can tumble down the sandy slope of ✳ Órthi Ámmos beach straight into the deep waters. There are only a few buildings along the entire coastal plain, and there is no centre as such, making it ideal for a relaxed, very quiet holiday. *F5*

TO EVERY MAN HIS WEAPON

Traffic signs are the favourite targets of some Cretans, which is why at least half of them on the island have holes in them. Stop or no-parking signs with holes in them are evidence of the Cretans' love of liberty. After all, traffic signs are a symbol of authority. According to statistics, every male on the island possesses at least one weapon, and yet violent crime is a rarity. The weapons are fired for joy at weddings and baptisms, or kept in case the Turks come back. The only thing they don't like is seeing policemen with weapons. When in 2011, hundreds of rapid response troops occupied the village of Zonianá in a raid on drug farmers and dealers, the people hit the streets in protest.

RÉTHIMNO

TWO COASTS & PLENTY IN BETWEEN

Double the fun. In Réthimno and the surrounding area, you will almost always have a view of not one, but two high mountain ranges: the White Mountains and the Ída Mountains. The two biggest island towns, Iráklio and Chaniá, are both only about an hour from Réthimno. And the road between the north and south coasts is extremely well developed, which means you can swim both in the Aegean and in the Libyan Sea in a single day.

Visit a restaurant on Réthimno's harbour at least once to soak up the unique atmosphere

There are pretty villages in the region's mountainous hinterland where you can easily spend half or even a whole day. Réthimno town, the regional capital, has something for everyone – with entertainment lasting well into the night.

A 16-km sandy beach with lots of water-sports options starts right on the edge of the old town which, with its numerous minarets and mosques, narrow streets and tiny squares, Venetian harbour and castle, is a lovely option worth leaving the beach for.

RÉTHIMNO

Kritikó

Venetian harbour ★
Réthimno
p. 60
Réthimno Beach
Ξηρόν Χωριόν
Xiro Chorio

Γεράνι
Gerani
Πρινές
Prines
Γάλλος
Gallos

Δράμια
Dramia

Επισκοπή
Episkopi

Ρουσσοσπίτι
Roussospiti

Γωνιά
Gonia
7 Arméni
Πρασιές
Prasies

Κούρνας
Kournas
Άγιος Κωνσταντίνος
Agios Kostantinos
Κάστελλος
Kastellos
Αρμένοι
Armeni
Σελλί
Selli

1 Argiroúpoli
Σαϊτούρες
Saitoures
Κούμοι
Koumi
Γουλεδιανά
Ghouledhiana
Potamón-
Stausee

Μυριοκέφαλα
Miriokefala
Βελόναδο
Velonado
Άγιος Βασίλειος
Agios Vasilios
Καρίνες
Karines

Αλώνες
Alonēs
Καλή Συκιά
Kali Sikia
Παλέ
Pale
Πα
Pa

Σελλιά
Sellia
Ατσιπάδες
Atsipades
8 Spíli

Κάτω Ροδάκινο
Kato Rodakino
Μύρθιος
Myrthios
Φρατί
Frati
Κίσ
Kis

11 Plakiás
9 Asómatos
Δριμίσκος
Drimiskos

Λευκώγεια
Lefkogia
Κεραμές
Kerames

Préveli ★ 10
Préveli Beach

🚲 47 km, 25 mins

🚗 47 km, 70 mins

Livikó

N
4 km
2.49 mi

Pélagos

Πέλαγος

Πάνορμος
Panormos

Σκεπαστή
Skepasti

Μπαλί
Bali

Ρουμελή
Roumeli

Εξάντης
Exandis

Βλυχάδα
Vlichada

ακάκι
kaki

Πρίνος
Prinos

90

Βιρανεπισκοπή
Viranepiskopi

Μελιδόνι 6

Μελιδόνι
Melidoni

Πέραμα
Perama

Αγιά
Agia

Αλφά
Alfa

15 km, 25 mins

Επισκοπή
Episkopi

Γαράζο
Garazo

Κάμπος Δοξαρού
Kambos Doxaru

5 Margarites

Αμνάτος
Amnatos

4 Eléftherna

Άγιος Μάμας
Agios Mamas

Άγιος Ιωάννης
Agios Ioannis

Αξός
Axos

Χάρκια
Charkia

3 Arkádi Monastery ★

Κάλυβος
Kalyvos

CRETE
ΚΡΗΤΗ

Ιαντάνασσα
Pantanassa

Αγία Φωτεινή
Agia Fotini

Βισταγή
Vistagi

MARCO POLO HIGHLIGHTS

★ VENETIAN HARBOUR
Crete's most beautiful harbour basin, lined with cafés and seafood tavernas ➤ p. 60

Αμάρι
Amari

ρακάρι
Gerakari

Μοναστηράκι
Monastiraki

★ ARKÁDI MONASTERY
This most famous of the island's monasteries is a national shrine ➤ p. 67

Βρύσες
Vrises

Βιζάρι
Vizari

Κουρούτες
Kouroutes

★ PRÉVELI
Two monasteries, a canyon and a dream of a beach – all very close together ➤ p. 70

ιος
s

Άνω Μέρος
Ano Meros

υμια
umia

Άγιος Ιωάννης
Agios Ioanis

Λοχριά
Lochria

Βορίζα
Voriza

Ορνέ
Orne

Αποδούλου
Apodoulou

Γρηγορία
Grigoria

Μάνδρες
Mandres

Κλημά
Klima

Λαγολιό
Lagolio

Μέλαμπες
Melambes

Καλοχωραφίτης
Kalochorafitis

12 Agía Galíni

Τυμπάκι
Tympaki

Φανερωμένη
Faneromeni

Three lion heads: the Venetian Rimóndi Fountain has been spouting water for 400 years

RÉTHIMNO

(🗺 H3) **There are endless shops and tavernas in Réthimno, and lots of pretty little streets take you through residential areas with quaint houses and the typical Turkish timber gazebos. In this town of a mere 55,000 inhabitants you won't have to spend long looking for good cocktail bars and clubs in the evenings; that's taken care of by the town's student scene. Public buses travel to many other towns and beaches in the surrounding area, while cruises along the coast start from the romantic harbour. So boredom is something you will definitely not have to contend with in Réthimno.**

Réthimno offers a number of cultural activities. The University of Crete has a campus here (as well as in Iráklio and Chaniá) and is home to the Philosophy Faculty – the city has seen itself as the intellectual centre of the island for a long time. Réthimno also has a theatre, a philharmonic society and an adult education college exclusively for women. During the summer months there are guest performances by local and foreign music and theatre groups.

SIGHTSEEING

VENETIAN HARBOUR ★
Even if you don't normally frequent fish restaurants, you have to eat at the old Venetian harbour at least once – ideally in the evening, when the buildings on the narrow, semi-circular quay look romantic rather than shabby, and the lighthouse dating back to Turkish times flashes a maritime

greeting. Tiny colourful fishing boats are tied up in front of all the tables and chairs outside the fish tavernas, leaving little space for people to walk past.

RIMÓNDI FOUNTAIN

The Venetian Rimondi Fountain is busiest during the day. The three stone lions' heads have been spouting water here since 1623. Four streets meet at the fountain, and anyone who is in Réthimno walks past at least once a day. It's the perfect spot to sit in a café and people-watch. *Platía Títu Peticháki*

ODÓS VERNÁRDOU

Looking for a "food boulevard"? In the evening and at night, you need to head for Odós Vernárdou. It has rows of typical rustic *rakádika*, all serving Cretan delights in small portions – just the way the locals like them. Live music is played, and later at night the street itself becomes a party venue. Sometimes you can break with the style and start the evening with classical music: there are occasional concerts in the town's *Odeon*, which is in an old mosque on Odós Vernárdou.

ARCHAEOLOGICAL MUSEUM

So just what is a loo seat doing in a museum? You'll find out when you visit this little archaeological exhibition in an old Venetian church. This particular loo seat is over 1,400 years old, made of stone, and was used for raising boat anchors that had stuck fast. Far more aesthetic are the painted sarcophagi that date back to Minoan times. Try to find the naked youth attempting to slay a boar with his sword. *Tue–Sun 10 am–6 pm | admission 2 euros | Odós Ethn. Antistáseos | ⏱ 15 mins*

MUSEUM OF CONTEMPORARY CRETAN ART

The island's best art museum not only has works by Cretan artists of the past 50 years, but also provides plenty of space for provocative contemporary exhibitions and performances. *Sat/Sun 10 am–3 pm, April–Oct Tue–Fri 9 am–2 pm and 7–9 pm, Nov–March Wed–Fri 9 am–2 pm, Wed, Fri also 6–9 pm | admission 3 euros | Odós Messolongíou 32 | cca.gr | ⏱ 20–30 mins*

FORTÉZZA

Time to catch your breath! Only the outer walls are left of the 16th-century Venetian castle. Inside, nature has reclaimed the vast plateau at the tip of the town peninsula. A chapel, a mosque and a few cisterns are the only historic traces that remain. The open-air stage is used for concerts and plays in summer, if there's enough money left in the town's coffers, that is. *May–Oct daily from 8.30 am–8 pm | admission 4 euros | ⏱ 1–1½ hrs*

EATING & DRINKING

AVLÍ

The finest cuisine in all of Réthimno. Cretan and Mediterranean dishes are served here with the slogan "nostalgic with a modern touch". Guests can sit in a courtyard adorned with flowers and under the arches of a Venetian town-house. The cellar is home to over 460 wines. *Daily from 7 pm | Odós Xanthoudidou 22 | tel. 28 31 05 82 50 | avli.gr | €€€*

KNOSSÓS

"Kráchtes" is what the Cretans call the waiters who talk to all the passers-by, attempting to lure them into their establishment.

There is only one landlady in the Venetian harbour who doesn't do this: María, in the smallest of all the tavernas, the Knossós. Her elderly mother still does the cooking, while María herself runs the service with plenty of charm, and her brother provides the entertainment with much clowning and plenty of music. The fish is served without frills or fuss from the grill, with oil and lemon as the only dressing. *Daily from noon | by the Venetian harbour | €€*

INSIDER TIP
Authentic and charming

LEMON TREE GARDEN

What do you do if you want to eat like the Cretans but there are only two of you? This establishment specialises in

In Odós Arkadíu you will find a huge selection of tablecloths and much more

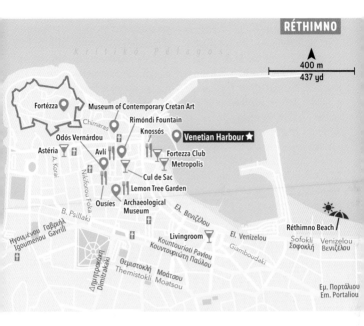

couples, so you can try a variety of Cretan specialities. There are various mixed starter platters or entire three-course meals with a wide range of delights. Vegetarian and vegan options are available on request. All meals are served under lemon and pomegranate trees. *Daily from 11 am | Odós Ethnikís Antistáseos 100 | €€*

OUSÍES 🚩

Of all the *rakádika* on the old town's "food boulevard", the Ousíes is the one with the most live Cretan music, namely the sounds of the *lýra* and *laoúto*. If you'd like to spend hours listening to it, you'll love the low price of the *rakí (2 euros / 0.2 litres)* and water pipe *(3.50 euros / hr)*. *Summer daily 11 am–2 am, winter daily 5 pm–2 am | Odós Vernárdou 20 | €€*

SHOPPING

The beautiful alley *Odós Arkadíu* in the old town is Réthimno's main shopping street. The locals also buy their shoes and clothes here. Souvenir shops can be found in Antistásseos, Súlion and Paleológou streets and the best Greek delicacies are at *Avlí* at *Armanpatzóglou 40 (Arabatzóglou)*.

SPORT & ACTIVITIES

The 16-km sandy beach starts right in the town centre. And it is here where *Ikarus (on the marina pier | tel. 69 70 09 96 23 | watersportikarus. com)* offers all kinds of water sports: jet skiing and water-skiing, parasailing and kite surfing, banana rides and, for the slightly more cautious, even pedalos. Mountain-biking needs are met by *Olympic Bike (Adelianós Kámbos 32 | tel. 28 31 07 27 83 | olympicbike.com)* on the beach promenade to the east of the town, while guided walks are provided by *Happy Walker (Odós Tombási 56 | tel. 28 31 05 29 20 | happywalker.com)*.

Great fun, especially for families, is to be had with trips on the 🎭 *Barbarossa motor boat (12–24 euros, for children as well | departing from the Venetian harbour | dolphin-cruises.com)* with its pirate ship design. The crew comprises buccaneers in full pirate garb, who engage with the children (who are also dressed up) and pose for photographs with them. Trips last from one to three hours.

BEACHES

🐦 Réthimno Beach is 16 km long and begins immediately behind the marina on the edge of the old town. This is where most of the resort hotels of the region are located. Regular bus services are ideal for getting to the beaches of Plakiás and Agía Galíni on the south coast.

WELLNESS

Participants in yoga and meditation courses on the south coast between Ágios Pávlos (⊞ H6) and Soúda (⊞ G5) may sense the earth's magical forces in this beautiful landscape. For details of what's on offer, please visit *yogatravelandbeyond.com*.

In the evening, Odós Vernárdo first becomes a food venue and then a party street

NIGHTLIFE

Where and when do things really get going? Well, before midnight head for *rakádika* in the Odós Vernárdou or the fabulously styled cocktail bars between the Venetian harbour and the marina. After midnight, the scene moves to the clubs in the short alleys right behind the Venetian harbour and the part of the Odós Salamínos near the marina.

ASTÉRIA

Open-air cinema and bar underneath the Venetian fortress walls. You'll be able to hear the likes of Brad Pitt, Angelina Jolie and other celebrities in their original language. But under the fabulous Cretan starry sky, even the biggest Hollywood celebrities are bound to shrink to the size of starlets. *Admission 7 euros | Odós Melisínu/ Odós Smírnis*

CUL DE SAC

The hotspot for warming up, right by the Rimondi Fountain. Also a good place for asking locals where the action will be tonight. *Platía Titu Peticháki 5–9 | culdesac.gr*

FORTEZZA CLUB

This is where many students spend the nights at the weekend, often till seven in the morning. The club plays modern Greek music. *Odós Neárchou 14*

LIVINGROOM

The trendy bar on the promenade serves everything the young Greek heart desires, from Greek coffee to French champagne as well as 18 different Greek wines by the glass and tasty ice cream sundaes. In typical Cretan fashion, guests receive a thirst-quenching glass of water before they order. *Odós Eleftheríou Venizélou 5 | livingroom.gr*

METROPOLIS

The disco classic with lots of parties. Mainstream music is popular. *Odós Neárchou 15 | in the Venetian harbour*

AROUND RÉTHIMNO

◪ ARGIROÚPOLI

21 km / 35 mins from Réthimno by car

Mountain villages don't have to be boring – you can easily spend a whole day in this one. It's best to start at the village church with its filigree clock tower. Right next door, a sign draws your attention to some old stone blocks: building remains of the antique town of Lappa, which once stood here. Diagonally opposite is the way into the old Venetian village. The archway is the first thing that will leave you speechless.

In the village you can buy all kinds of hand creams, gels and lotions made from avocados, which have been grown in the region since the 1990s. You can also get a free map of the town in the shop. The nameless *kafenío* is a nice place to drink a coffee or avocado juice and eat avocado and

Arkádi Monastery: once a battleground, but today it is all peace and quiet

shrimps. An approximately 30-minute tour of the village takes you to a lovely Roman floor mosaic and the photogenic little chapel of *Agía Paraskeví*. The step down to the churchyard is, in fact, the lid of an antique child-sized sacrophagus. The surrounding unspoilt countryside is, sprinkled with ancient graves. Follow the signs on the little road to Káto Póros 400 m further, and then to the "Holy 5 Virgins". These little *rock graves* are about 2,000 years old.

For lunch, trout and sturgeon, freshly caught in the gushing springs, await you in the tavernas. To dine in a historic ambience, head for *Au Vieux Moulin (daily from 11 am | €€)*, set in and around an old water mill. On the way back to Réthimno, you can stop at the modern shop, which makes innovative use of another traditional natural product: carob. At the *Creta Carob Shop (cretacarob.com)*, you will find all sorts of natural products made from carob, from syrup to tea, coffee and cocoa. ⚏ *G4*

2 POTAMÓN RESERVOIR

21 km / 35 mins from Réthimno by car

For nine months in 2014/15, a 2-m crocodile known as "Sifis" swam in Crete's newest reservoir. No one knew where it had come from, but then it was found dead after a cold winter, floating on the water. It is still talked about at the *Café Potamon (daily from 10 am | €)* on the 310-m long dam wall, and the creature's plastic brother hangs from the ceiling. Something wonderful awaits you at *Ágios Antónios Gorge* in the nearby village of Pátsos. Start at the large,

generously signposted forest taverna *Drymos (daily from 10 am | €)*, where lovers of hearty meat dishes find plenty of (affordable) dishes, as do vegetarians with a taste for the unusual. Just a five-minute walk later, you'll be in the gorge gazing in at the *tiny cave chapel of St Antónios* with fascinating examples of the Orthodox belief in miracles: notes with prayers have been slipped into cracks in the rocks; romper suits hang inside the church, and crutches have been placed in the corners. 🕮 *H4*

3 ARKÁDI MONASTERY ★
23 km / 40 mins from Réthimno by car

Can mass suicide be a heroic deed? Crete's clear answer to that is "yes". Which is why the monastery on an isolated high plain has been declared a national shrine of the island. In 1866, Cretan insurgents were entrenched here, together with their wives and children, against approaching Turkish troops. When, after a two-day siege, the Turks broke into the monastery, the insurgents all gathered in the powder magazine and blew themselves up rather than face rape and enslavement. Over 900 Christians died. The story of this "heroic" suicide quickly spread throughout the world, and ultimately led to Crete being annexed to the Greek motherland in 1913. The bones and skulls of numerous victims are now on display in glass cabinets in the *Mausoleum* opposite the entrance to the monastery. Flowers are still placed on an altar in the now-roofless powder magazine, while the story of Arkádis is told in more detail in the *Monastery Museum (May, Sept, Oct daily 9 am–7 pm, June–Aug daily 9 am–8 pm, otherwise daily 9 am–5 pm | admission 3 euros).* 🕮 *J4*

4 ELÉFTHERNA
22 km / 40 mins from Réthimno by car

Since the Minoans were immigrants from Asia rather than being Greek, the excavations at Eléftherna are extremely important to today's Cretans. Genuine Hellenes lived here 2,000–3,000 years ago, something that is also emphasised in the state-of-the-art *Museum (Tue–Sun 10 am–6 pm | admission 4 euros)*, which opened in 2016. It is also confirmed by the *three archaeological sites* that you can explore on a half-day hike from here if they are still accessible and haven't

A clay bird-feeder handmade in Margarítes

in Margarítes. More than 20 ceramicists work here in studios along the village street, producing objects of art and kitsch, useful things or simply pretty things. In the midst of them all, landlady Eléni prepares her legendary moussaká fresh every morning at *Gianousákis (daily from 10 am | €)*. ⟮ J4

⑥ MELIDÓNI

31 km / 45 mins from Réthimno by car

Now you have to be brave. That's because the latest attraction in this pretty, old village is 👕 *Reptisland (summer daily 8 am–8 pm, winter daily 9 am–3 pm | admission 3 euros | next to the petrol station at the north entrance to the village)*, with scorpions, tarantulas, frogs, lizards and giant snakes from all over the world. The Papakostánti brothers, whose animals they are, will be pleased to place the frog on your hand for you to waken with a kiss – or, if you prefer, you can wrap a 5-m python around your shoulders. If you would then like to relax, you can drive up to the *Melidóni sta-lactite cave (daily 8 am until sunset | admission 4 euros)*, which is only 2 km away. The bones and skulls on the altar that commemorate a Turkish massacre in 1824 will hardly alarm you now. On the side of the road into the neighbouring village of Agía you'll see charcoal burners, who still produce charcoal the traditional way in piles under the open sky. If you would like to take something with you to remind you of this special place, go to the modern 🐖 *Paráskákis olive oil*

been closed due to lack of funds (check in advance at the museum). For

INSIDER TIP
Mapping the past

an excellent map of the entire ancient town, visit short.travel/ kre9. And you will need it! By the way, you can explore antique cisterns in the neighbouring village of Archéa Eléftherna, which is quite good fun. ⟮ J4

⑤ MARGARÍTES 👕

27 km / 40 mins from Réthimno by car

Are you still looking for a few souvenirs? You'll find an excellent selection factory (open daily | admission free) on the road to Pérama.

INSIDER TIP
With open arms

Owner Ioánna and her mother are very friendly and only too happy to answer any questions you may have about Crete. Those who buy their olive oil here will carry these memories forever. *K3*

7 ARMÉNI

6 km / 15 mins from Réthimno by car

Crete's prettiest cemetery is situated in a forest of kermes and vallonea oaks. Over the past 50 years, archaeologists have excavated more than 230 tombs. The deceased were buried there about 3,300 years ago. The tombs are all of different sizes, and you can enter many of them. It's not at all spooky; in fact, it's actually a great setting for a picnic in the countryside.

April–Oct Tue–Sun 10 am–6 pm, Nov–March Tue–Sun 8 am–3 pm | admission 3 euros | *H4*

8 SPÍLI

30 km / 45 mins from Réthimno by car

On the drive between the north and south coasts, stop at the large, old mountain village of Spíli. Have coffee on the shady *platía* with water bubbling forcefully from the numerous lions' heads of its Venetian fountain, and then drive on. *H5*

9 ASÓMATOS

30 km / 40 mins from Réthimno by car

The village priest Michális Georgioulákis (1921–2008) always did everything differently and consequently his village museum *Oriseum (daily 10 am–5 pm | admission*

The cisterns of Archéa Eléftherna were carved out of the rock 2,300 years ago

3.50 euros) is unique. On display is everything that he collected from surrounding villages, bought at flea markets or inherited over 60 years. ⟳ *H5*

10 PRÉVELI ★

37 km / 1 hr from Réthimno by car

You can spend an entire day of your holiday at Préveli. There is the terrific *Préveli Beach*, a lovely taverna, an old bridge, two monasteries and a canyon full of palm trees – short walk included. Coming from the main road, after 2 km you first cross a photogenic bridge with a lovely arch that farmers used to cross with their donkeys. By the rushing mountain stream below is a good *taverna (daily from 10 am | €)* with ducks outside that you can feed. A further 600 m below the road are the accessible ruins of the *Káto Préveli Monastery*. The road ends 3.2 km further on at the *Piso Préveli Monastery (25 March–May daily 9 am–7 pm, June–Oct Mon–Sat 9 am–1.30 pm and 3.30–7 pm, Sun 9 am–7 pm | admission 2.50 euros).* In 1941, the monks hid British soldiers here until they could be picked up by submarines.

Between Káto and Píso Préveli, a cul-de-sac branches off towards the coast, and ends at a car park *(2 euros/ day).* A steep footpath takes you from there down to the Préveli stream in about 30 minutes. A river with cold water flows across the beach (about 200 m long) into the sea from the Kourtaliátiko Gorge, a narrow canyon overgrown by palm trees. You might be able to manage the walk towards

the source as far as the taverna with the ducks. You will have to clamber over rapids and rocks, wade through knee-high or chest-high water and, at certain places, you even have to swim. ⟳ *H5*

11 PLAKIÁS

40 km / 1 hr from Réthimno by car

The *sandy beach* at Plakiás is over 800 m long, and widens to the west into a dune landscape – where you can also obtain an all-over tan if you so want. Almost all of the bars and tavernas are right beside the water, and there are daily boat trips out from the tiny harbour to *Préveli Beach*. Signposted hiking trails lead through olive groves, past old water mills and up into the mountain villages of *Mýrthios* and *Selliá*, where you will find craft shops as well as good tavernas. There is affordable jewellery in Mýrthios from Josíf Petrákis at the *Líthos Nature Collection*, and in Selliá from Jánnis and Angelika at the *Ikaros*. *Carola Poppinga* from Germany makes guardian angels from alpaca wire in Selliá, while *Jánnis Méxis* and *Pinélopi Kostogiánni* shape fabulous items out of wood and modelling clay in Mýrthios. The *Anso* travel agency organises guided tours and mountain-bike rides. ⟳ *G5*

12 AGÍA GALÍNI

55 km / 75 mins from Réthimno by car

If you are anything but shy, then you'll feel completely at home in this village, which has the pretty name of "Holy Tranquillity". The densely built centre stretches from the harbour up a

There are easy hikes from Plakiás to the villages of Selliá and Mýrthios

narrow valley that has most of the hotels and guesthouses on its slopes. The actual centre is formed by three vertical and two horizontal streets full of shops, bars and cafés. Most of the tavernas reach up several floors right next to the harbour square, their roof gardens and terraces sparkling with lights in the evenings between the sky and the sea. All village life happens in an area measuring about 100 x 200 m, so you'll keep meeting the same people. A good place for a rendezvous is the modern memorial to the mythical aviators Daedalus and Icarus on the terrace above the harbour. There's swimming off a long, narrow beach 200 m to the north of the harbour. And throughout the day several boats head out to the beaches in the area and as far as *Préveli Beach* (see p. 70). Delicious Cretan food is served at taverna *Ílios (€€)*, near the bus stop. 🕮 J6

IRÁKLIO

THE HEARTBEAT OF THE ISLAND

Landed safely? Every year, more than six million passengers land at Iráklio (Heraklion) airport, and more than one-third of all Cretans live in the city's greater metropolitan area. From a distance, Iráklio (city) (pop. almost 200,000) may look like an urban sprawl, but fear not! The city centre is pretty, clearly laid out and, above all, bursting with urban life. By day and night.

Large hotels are centred on the northern coast between Heraklion and Mália, but even these resorts don't compare to the kind of mass

Having a chat: the entire city meets at the Morosíni Fountain

tourism that is found on the coasts of other countries. And, on the southern coast, independent travellers will feel completely at home. Between the two coasts are vineyards, the fertile Messará Plain and two wild mountain ranges. Excursions take you back 3,500 years to the Minoan palace towns of Festós and Knossós, where were the centres of Europe's first advanced civilisation. The remains of five-storey houses can still be seen, and the unique artefacts discovered at these sites are on display in the Archaeological Museum in Iráklio.

IRÁKLIO

Kritikó Pélagos

Nisí Día

Σκεπαστή
Skepasti

Μπαλί
Bali

Σίσσες
Sisses

Αχλάδα
Achlada

Φόδελε 7
Fódele

Παλαιόκαστρο
Paliokastro

Archaeological Museum ★

Πέραμα
Perama

Γαράζο
Garazo

Δροσιά
Drosiá

Δαμάστα
Damasta

Ammoudará Beach

Γάζι
Gazi

Iráklio
p. 76

Λιβάδια
Livadia

Αξός
Axos

Γωνιές
Gónies

4 Τίλισσος
Tílissos

Knossós ★ 1

Zonianá 6

5 Ανώγια
Anógia

Καμάρι
Kamari

Σταυράκια
Stavrakia

Σκαλ
Skalá

Φουρφουράς
Fourfouras

Αγιος Μύρωνας
Agios Mironas

Αρχάνες
Arehanes

Κουρούτες
Kouroutes

Κάτω Ασίτες
Kato Asites

32 km, 30 mins

Χουδέτσι
Choudhetsi

Αποδούλου
Apodoulou

55 km, 80 mins

Παρθένι
Partheni

Αλ
A

Αγία Γαλήνη
Agia Galini

Zarós 13

Μακρές
Makres

CRETE
ΚΡΗΤΗ

Τυμπάκι
Tympaki

11 Vóri

9 **Festós** ★ 10 Mires

Γόρτις 12
Górtis

Άγιοι Δέκα
Agii Deka

Στόλοι
Stoli

100 km, 120 m

Πρετόρι
Protoria

Κόμο Beach

8 Pitsídia

Πετροκεφάλι
Petrokefali

Πλάτανος
Platanos

Στέρνες
Sternes

Πύργος
Pyrgos

Red Beach

Mátala ★
p. 86

Πηγαιδάκια
Pigaidakia

Άγιος Κύριλλος
Agios Kyrillos

Παράνυμφοι
Paranimfi

Λέντας
Lentas

Livikó

10 km
6.21 mi

MARCO POLO HIGHLIGHTS

★ **ARCHAEOLOGICAL MUSEUM**
Treasures of the Minoan civilisation
➤ p. 76

★ **KNOSSÓS**
Captivating ruins of archaeology's
"Disneyland" ➤ p. 82

★ **MÁTALA**
Hippie caves, old fishing village, sandy
beaches – it's easy to get lost in your
memories ➤ p. 86

★ **FESTÓS**
A Minoan palace with a fantastic view
➤ p. 88

IRÁKLIO

(M–N4) **Road traffic has been brought well under control in recent years; traffic lights have been removed and many pedestrian precincts created, which means there is now even more room for tavernas and street cafés. Iráklio has the best shopping on the island; its museums are among the most important in Greece, and there is much to discover from Venetian times.**

SIGHTSEEING

ARCHAEOLOGICAL MUSEUM ★

If not here, then where? The two-storey museum contains more finds from Minoan times than all of the other museums in the world combined. And as well as noble art, it also contains numerous items that speak to us of everyday life here – about 3,500 years ago. On display are Minoan house façades made from tiles, a board game, clay model ships and houses, jewellery and a number of seals. One of the most valuable pieces is a vessel in the shape of a bull's head carved from soapstone with rock crystal eyes and a mother of pearl mouth; another is a rhyton, a drinking and alms vessel made of shimmering rock crystal. The 3,500-year-old Phaistos disc is particularly fascinating. It is covered on both sides with a spiral of 241 hieroglyphics stamped into the clay, the meaning of which has never been conclusively explained. The murals in the Palace of

Knossós and the Minoan villas are staggeringly beautiful – they look like prehistoric photo wallpaper. *April–Oct daily 8 am–8 pm, Nov–March Mon 11 am–5 pm, Tue–Sun 8 am–3 pm | admission 10 euros (Nov–March 5 euros), combined ticket with Knossós 16 euros (8 euros), tickets online at etickets.tap.gr | Platía Eleftherías/Odós Xanthudínu | ⏱ 1½–2 hrs*

KOULES FORTRESS

This will get your blood flowing. First you climb under the dark arches of the Venetian harbour fort and up onto the roof to look out over the old town to the Cretan mountains. Then you can join the joggers running a circuit along the approx. 1-km pier. *Tue–Sun 8 am–3 pm | admission 3 euros | at the pier of the fishing harbour | ⏱ 15–25 mins*

WHERE TO START?

Venetian harbour: In order to avoid the problem of finding parking in Iráklio, it is best to go there by bus. If you arrive by car, you can park along the shore at the commercial port (partly free), then walk in a westerly direction for about five to 15 minutes to the Venetian harbour on the edge of the old town.

ÁGIOS TÍTOS CHURCH

Holy hoo-ha? Many Cretans would beg to differ. They believe that the skull in the silver reliquary in the side chapel on the left really is that of St

The Venetian fort was built to keep intruders out, but proved an insufficient defence

Titus, the island's first bishop almost 2,000 years ago. *Daily 7 am–noon and 5 pm–8 pm | admission free | Odós 25 Avgústu |* ⏱ *5–10 mins*

ÁGIOS MÁRKOS CATHEDRAL

The oldest Venetian church built in 1239 (close to the *Morosíni Fountain*) today hosts concerts and exhibitions. The monolithic pillars of the basilica date back to ancient times. *Opening times vary | admission free | Odós 25 Avgústu |* ⏱ *10–15 mins*

MOROSÍNI FOUNTAIN

Arranging somewhere to meet? The Venetian "lion" fountain is the general meeting place of the city. It's where all the main day- and night-time streets come together: the wide pedestrian street is 25 Avgústou, the main shopping streets are Dédalu, 1866 and Kalokerinú, and the nightlife areas are Handakós and Platía Korái. The fountain square itself is perfect for a *gyros* in the hand or a *bugátsa* in a café, with people from all over the world as a source of constant entertainment. *Platía Venizélou*

ODÓS 1866

Although the 200-m street is no longer a traditional market for locals, there's still plenty going on. It's an excellent place to shop for culinary souvenirs, to pop into rather old-fashioned tavernas and *kafenía* or modern bistros and coffee shops. The best place to sit is at the eastern end of the street beside the Venetian Bembo Fountain, which is adorned by a headless statue.

ÁGIOS MINÁS CATHEDRAL

Do you like looking through colourful picture books? The cathedral of Iráklio, about 150 years old, is just that – a picture book that up to 8,000 people can read at the same time. Cupolas, arches and walls are completely covered in paintings of numerous biblical stories.

INSIDER TIP
A different kind of quiz

Turn it into a game, and try to find the story of the birth of Jesus and his crucifixion. Any others that you find will certainly earn you additional points in heaven! *Usually open during the day | admission free | Platía Agía Ekaterínis | ⓘ 10–15 mins*

MUSEUM OF CHRISTIAN ART

Icons are not for everyone, but for those who do appreciate them, here are six masterpieces by Michaíl Damaskinós, the most important representative of the Cretan style of holy art in the 16th century. *April–Oct daily 9.30 am–7.30 pm, Nov–March daily 9.30 am–6 pm | admission 4 euros | Platía Ekaterínis | ⓘ 15–25 mins*

HISTORICAL MUSEUM

What did Iráklio look like 400 years ago? A large wooden model shows it clearly at a scale of 1:500. Also interesting are the medieval hand grenades made of glass and ceramic; Cretan folk costumes and art; an office of the *Sorbás* author Níkos Kazantzákis; and for art lovers, two small paintings by El Greco. *Mon–Sat 9 am–5 pm, winter until 3.30 pm | admission 5 euros | Odós Lysimachou Kalokerinou 7 | historical-museum.gr | ⓘ 20–30 mins*

Images from the more recent past: ceiling frescoes in Iráklio's Ágios Minás Cathedral

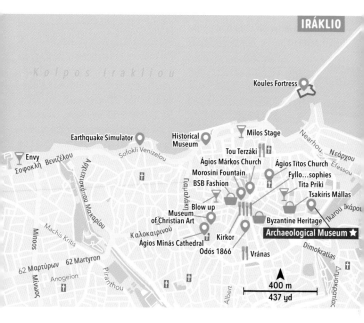

IRÁKLIO

Kolpos Irakliou

Koules Fortress

Earthquake Simulator

Envy

Σοφοκλή Βενιζέλου

Αρχιεπισκόπου Μακαρίου

Minoos

Machis Kritis

62 Μαρτύρων 62 Martyron

Μίνωος

Anogeion

Sofokli Venizélou

Historical Museum

Milos Stage

Tou Terzáki

Ágios Márkos Church

Morosini Fountain

BSB Fashion

Blow up

Museum of Christian Art

Καλοκαιρινού

Ágios Minás Cathedral

Kirkor

Odós 1866

Nearhou Νεάρχου

Ágios Títos Church

Fyllo...sophies

Tita Priki

Tsakiris Mállas

Byzantine Heritage

Archaeological Museum ★

Vránas

Dimokratias

Piranthou

Albert

Nέαρχου

Εφέσσου

Ικάρου Ικάρου

Δημοκρατίας

400 m
437 yd

EARTHQUAKE SIMULATOR ☂

What does it feel like when the earth quakes? That is something that no one would really want to experience, but in the simulator of the *Museum of Natural History* it's both interesting and perfectly safe. In a replica of an old classroom, earthquakes of various forces give you a good shaking every half-hour. *Mon–Fri 9 am–9 pm, Sat/Sun 10 am–9 pm | admission 9 euros | Leof. Sof. Venizélou | nhmc.uoc.gr*

EATING & DRINKING

KIRKOR / FYLLO...SOPHIES

Fancy something sweet? These two cafés serve *bougátsa*, a type of semolina pudding with filo pastry, dusted with lots of icing sugar. Make sure to eat it over a napkin, otherwise you will

look as if it has snowed! A savoury version is the *bougátsa tirí* made with a sheep's cheese filling. *Daily from 6 am | Morosini Fountain | €*

TOU TERZÁKI

Help wanted! Because Cretans like to spend a long time discussing what to eat with everyone else at the table, an old custom is coming back into fashion: the waiter presents the guests with a list instead of a menu, and they then put a cross by all the things they'd like to eat. There are plenty of unusual dishes as well as all the usuals – why not try Cretan snails? *Daily from 11 am, Sun in winter from 6 pm | Odós Marinélli 17 | €€*

VRÁNAS

Fish doesn't come any fresher than in

this small taverna on the edge of the fish market in Iráklio. Watch what happens when you order fish for lunch: the landlord shouts your order to the fishmonger across the lane who promptly delivers it to the kitchen. *Mon–Sat 11 am to midnight | Odós Karteroú 13 | tel. 28 10 28 85 54 | €*

INSIDER TIP
Straight from the net into the pan

SHOPPING

BSB FASHION

BSB is one of the biggest fashion companies in Greece and is currently expanding worldwide and on the web. From denim to festive, metallic to the office – there's plenty of choice, and it's different from what you normally find at home! *Odós Idís 26–28 | bsbfashion.com*

BYZANTINE HERITAGE

You'll find silver-plated fashion jewellery from as little as 7 euros in this shop on the market street, and almost nothing over 50 euros. What's lovely is that you can tell by the designs that the charming gifts were made in Greece. *Odós 1866*

TSAKÍRIS MÁLLAS

Art for the feet: the women of Crete love going out in the most progressive shoes, sandals and boots made by Greek shoe artists – but there's also plenty on offer for the more conservative, as well as for men and children, all usually at reasonable prices. *Odós Dédalu 30–32 | tsakirismallas.gr*

SPORT & ACTIVITIES

The most common types of water sport are available on the city beaches of Iráklio. Wonderful outings for families include the 🐟 *Cretaquarium (May–Sept daily 9.30 am–9 pm, otherwise until 5 pm | admission 9 euros, Nov–April 6 euros, children (aged 5–17) 6 euros | cretaquarium.gr)* and the 🦕 *Dinosauria Park (May–Sept daily 10 am–8 pm, Nov–April Sat/Sun 10 am–5 pm | admission 19 euros, children (aged 4–12) 8 euros | dinosauriapark.com)*, both of which are in nearby Goúrnes.

BEACHES

Are you getting too hot in the city? *Municipal buses (astiko-irakleiou.gr)* take you to the nearby beaches for a very small fee: Line 6 leaves from the bus terminal by the harbour and runs to long ⛱ sandy beaches at Ammoudára, while Line 7 leaves from the Platía Eleftherías in front of the Archaeological Museum and runs to the ⛱ sandy beach of Amnissós.

WELLNESS

DOCTOR FISH SPA

Are your feet sore yet from all the sightseeing? Doctor Fish Spa offers soothing treatments from more than 100 little fish which nibble on your hard skin and may make you feel rather ticklish. *Daily. 10 am–9 pm | Odós 25is Avgoústou 13 | tel. 28 10 28 78 79 | doctorfish.gr*

When Cretans go "into town", they mean shopping in the old town of Iráklio

NIGHTLIFE

In the evenings young Iráklion people meet in the bars and music cafés at *Platía Korái,* while a more alternative crowd frequent the little bars in the *Odós Chandakós.* Dance clubs open around midnight in *Odós Epimenídu* and at the western edge of the old town on the coastal road *S. Venizélu.*

BLOW UP

More of a pub with music than a bar, and more alternative than mainstream. Lots of students. DJs every evening, sometimes soul, blues and funk live. It's a good place to talk to people as well. *Daily from 8 pm | 15 Odós Psaromilíngon*

ENVY CLUB

Disco like at home? That would be the Envy Club, a firm fixture in the city's young nightlife scene. There's often live Greek rock music in summer, when you'll have to pay for admission *(20 euros including 1 drink). Daily from 11 pm | Leof. Sof. Venizélou | Tálos Centre*

MILOS STAGE

Critics describe the live Greek music that is played here at weekends and attracts up to 300 fans as *skiládika* – like howling dogs with something to celebrate. This is the place to go if you want to see Cretans relaxed and dancing Greek dances. The place really starts buzzing after 1 am. *Fri/Sat from 11.30 pm | Odós Lachaná/Mitsotáki | tel. for bookings 69 36 78 77 10*

TITA PRIKI

Around midnight this usually quite normal bar turns into party central for singles. Admission is free, the music Greek and international. *Daily from noon | Odós Mirabélu 8*

AROUND IRÁKLIO

1 KNOSSÓS ★

5 km / 10 mins from Iráklio by bus

The no. 1 of the island's top sights. Over 3,500 years ago, the so-called Palace of Knossós was already a major town with a population of perhaps 80,000. While the rest of us were still living in caves, some people in Knossós were living in four-storey houses with sewage systems, paved roads and squares. Pretty frescoes adorned the walls, and works of art of a unique elegance were created in workshops, while the people stored provisions in vast jugs in storage rooms. And although the people of Knossós used a form of writing, they did so mainly for recording the dates of their stores and provisions; they passed nothing of themselves and their history on to us.

The Englishman Sir Arthur Evans unearthed the settlement in the first quarter of the 20th century – and then rebuilt it in sections which is why, unlike in other places, you can see more than just a few layouts and walls. Columns and pillars support many a roof, and murals adorn the walls. You will be able to imagine life in those ancient times. Also of help are the postcards with the coloured reconstruction drawing of the whole complex, which you can buy near the cash desk.

The "palace" was without doubt a multipurpose building. Religious ceremonies played a large part. In festivals, processions progressed through long corridors, as can be seen in the frescoes on the wall of the west corridor at the beginning of a tour. They were heading for the large central courtyard. Adjoining it to the west are a number of dark halls, such as the pillar crypts, which imitate cave sanctuaries. Sir Arthur even found a kind of throne in one room. Perhaps it was left unoccupied for a deity, or perhaps it was used by a priestess. He believed it might have been reserved for the legendary king. He also believed he had found, in the former four-storey building on the eastern side of the central courtyard, the rooms of the king and queen, both of which had a water closet, although there is some doubt about this today. It is more likely to have been a building with luxury apartments. *April–Oct daily 8 am–8 pm, Nov–March 8 am–3 pm | admission 15 euros, combi-ticket with Archaeological Museum Iráklio 16 euros | online tickets available at etickets.tap.gr | From Iráklio the city bus no. 2 leaves from the bus station at the harbour and from the bus stop in front of house no. 62 in Odos 1821, every 20 mins to Knossós, which is only 5 km away. ⊞ N4*

2 CHERSÓNISOS

26 km / 25 mins from Iráklio by car

This is where it's at! *Liménas Chersónisou* is the international party metropolis on the island. The traffic-free beach promenade is almost 2 km long with lots of tavernas, café bars, pubs and music clubs. About

200 m from the beach is the equally long main street with hundreds of shops and more pubs and restaurants. It's never boring here, which is why people are also happy to accept that in the town itself, there is too little beach for too many people. Instead, they use the many hotel pools or the ☛ *Star Beach Water Park (admission free)* on the northern outskirts of the town with its water slides and party sounds that start in the morning.

When you want to escape from the noise and bustle, head to the mountainside villages of *Koutouloufári* and *Piskopianó*, which are about 20 minutes away. With their narrow streets and natural brick buildings, they are every bit as idyllic as you probably expected Crete to be. You can easily spend an evening in the elegant cocktail bars. A good "Cretan village evening" *(Mon from 8 pm | €€)* with music and folk dancing is organised by the innkeepers at the tavernas on the *platía* of the nearby village of Chersónisos. (Until 50 years ago, Liménas Chersónisou was merely a poor boat mooring for the village.) If you want to learn about life on Crete before the tourists came, visit the private open-air museum *Lychnostátis (Sun–Fri 9 am–2 pm | admission 6 euros)* on the eastern outskirts of the town. Its exhibits are informative and an extremely entertaining.

INSIDER TIP
Greek entertainment

If you are keen to learn about Minoan culture, start with the Palace of Knossós

3 MÁLIA

37 km / 35 mins from Iráklio by car

This expansive holiday resort is usually firmly in the hands of young British visitors. Nowhere else are the screens in the sports bars bigger, the quads more numerous on the streets, and the tattoo studios open longer at night. Shots and beer flow freely – and yet potatoes still thrive in the deep-red fields among all the bars, clubs and hotels.

The fine ✈ sandy beach is lovely and wide, and miles long. If you stay at one of the better hotels, you'll hardly notice all the noise and bustle. And if you find yourself wanting to see the more traditional Crete, stroll through old Mália on the other side of the main road, where the taverna *Kalesma (daily from 6.30 pm | Odós Omirú 8 | €€€)* still serves traditional Cretan cuisine. Lovers of ancient ruins won't want to miss the *Minoan Palace of Mália (Tue–Sun 8 am–3 pm | admission 6 euros)* on the eastern edge of the town. It was the third biggest palace on Crete 3,500 years ago. ⊞ P4

4 TÍLISSOS

15 km / 25 mins from Iráklio by car

Would you like a romantic breather? Then head for the little-visited excavations of three Minoan country houses on the edge of the village today. The old pine trees will provide you and the 3,500-year-old walls with plenty of shade.

Flowering capers climb up the walls in the early summer. Cicadas will perform a private concert for you as you snooze in the grass. And once again, you'll be amazed by the exceptionally highly developed architecture of the Minoans: water pipes lead to the former two-storey buildings, feeding a cistern. Vast, lavishly decorated storage containers are dotted about, some of them still almost intact. *Daily 9 am–4 pm | admission 2 euros | ⊞ M4*

5 ANÓGIA

43 km / 1 hr from Iráklio by car

Where does the heart of "real Crete" beat? Most locals will agree that it's in Anógia, where they mostly listen to the traditional Cretan music of the Xyloúris family. Widely regarded as the musical royal family of the island, the Xyloúris family hail from Anógia and their main home in the lower *platía* of the village is now a *museum (open during the day | admission free)*. In the minds of the Cretans, Anógia is the symbol of the resistance to the German occupiers in World War II: in 1944, they burnt the town down as punishment for the embarrassing abduction of their General Heinrich Kreipe to Egypt, and shot all the men they could find in the village. This is commemorated in a plaque and memorial near the town hall in the upper part of the village. Scenes of the occupation and resistance were also the main themes of the naïve village painter, whose work can be seen in the *Museum of Alkiwíades Skulás Grílios (key at the Kafeníon Skulás | admission free)* near the lower village square.

However, today one of the main reasons Anógia is considered the "heart of Crete" is because it is home

For many Cretans, picturesque Anógia is the most symbolic place on the island

to the island's biggest flocks of sheep and goats. Over 100,000 animals provide milk, cheese and meat and they graze mainly on the common land of the uninhabited ► *Nída Plateau* at the foot of the Psilorítis Mountains, which is reached by a 21-km road. Many Cretans come to the tavernas of Anógia for their meat at the weekends in particular. *Gagáris (daily from 10 am | €€)* in the upper part of the village on the one-way street down is good. *L4*

6 ZONIANÁ
43 km / 1 hr from Iráklio by car
The mountain village is considered the centre of Crete's hemp cultivation, which frequently leads to police raids. But if you don't act like a secret police-man or photo reporter, you'll find the village as harmless and peaceful as all the others, if perhaps a little poorer. There's also something to see: on the outskirts of the village is the 550-m long ⚓ *Sventóni stalactite cave (April–Oct daily from 10.30 am–5 pm, Nov–March only Sat/Sun 10.30 am–2.30 pm | admission 4 euros | zoniana.gr)*. Directly on the platía is the *Potamiós waxwork museum (summer daily 10 am–7 pm, winter 10 am–5.30 pm | admission 5 euros)*, with reproductions à la Madame Tussaud of important events in the history of Crete, from Minos to today. *K4*

7 FÓDELE
29 km / 40 mins from Iráklio by car
Interested in art? In this village in between orange and olive groves the

painter Doménikos Theotokópulos was born in 1541. He later became known worldwide as El Greco. The home in which he was born *(May–Oct daily 9 am–7 pm | admission 2.50 euros)* has been wonderfully reconstructed. A lovely *kafenío* and a church from the tenth century are in front of it. The church has a mosaic depicting fishermen at work. 〰 *L3*

MÁTALA

(〰 K7) **Today is life. Tomorrow never comes! That was and is the motto of the former fishing village of ★ Mátala on the south coast.** During the Vietnam War, Mátala made a name for itself as a stronghold for hippies. Today the annual *Mátala Beach Festival*, which takes place around Whitsun, reawakens old memories. During the rest of the summer, hippie flair combines with day visitors and the usual holidaymakers. Now, the curious visitors scramble around the *caves (daily 8 am–3 pm | admission 2 euros)* in the rock wall on the north side of the bay that were once burial sites for the Romans and then, centuries later, homes for the flower children. In the few buildings and boat sheds on the south side of the old fishing settlement, people dine in rustic fish tavernas before enjoying the night in cool hammocks or tiny music clubs. Between the two shores is a wide sandy beach some 200 m long, and behind that a short bazaar alley that is still a little like a north African souk.

Today, the hippie caves in the cliffs of Mátala are uninhabited, but the cove is still a draw

EATING & DRINKING

AKUNA MATATA

The name is Swahili, and sums up the venue: no problems. Cool location on the water, psychedelic colours, 1970s atmosphere and music. Flower power times – almost as if you were there. Except that back then, people didn't drink cocktails or eat finger food or scampi, and they still made their own music. *Daily from 11 am | old fishing quarter | €–€€*

MYSTICAL VIEW

The view makes the difference: you sit high above Kómo Beach here, overlooking Psilorítis and watching the sun sink into the sea. It's almost mystical. *Signposted on the road to Pitsídia, approx. 2.5 km from Mátala | €€*

SHOPPING

AXEL GENTHNER

In the shop and studio of this gold- and silversmith who settled in Mátala long ago, you'll find the kind of jewellery that no one else is wearing. *Sun-Fri 1–7 pm | main street, in the shopping area at the Hotel Zafiria | matala-jewellery.de*

BEACHES

KÓMO BEACH ✶⋆

Over 2 km long and 40 m wide, there's a taverna at the southern end and a small town right at the north. Otherwise you'll just find sand that you don't have to have bathing trunks or a bikini for. Unfortunately, it's 3 km from Mátala, but then that's what mopeds are for.

MÁTALA BEACH

The beach for comfort-lovers, right in town. Full in summer, but relaxed. Hardly any recliners for hire, but people bring their own beach towels.

RED BEACH ✶⋆

The red shimmering beach is a 30-minute walk from the village. Almost as far from civilisation as in the old hippie days.

NIGHTLIFE

PORT SIDE

DJs play until 5 am, and occasionally there's live music right beside the sea. Breakfast is from 8 am – and in between, go for a swim. *Old fishing quarter*

AROUND MÁTALA

8 PITSÍDIA

4 km / 10 mins from Mátala by car

Are you more the backpack type of tourist? Then the cosy *platía* of this little inland village is just the place for you. The *Café Synántisi (daily from 8 am | €)* has been a meeting place for relaxed guests (who often bring their own guitar or lyre with them) for generations. It's easy to hitchhike to Mátala and Kómo Beach, which is about 2.5 km away. *K6*

9 FESTÓS ★

10 km / 15 mins from Mátala by car

First Knossós, then Festós – that's the correct sequence for the two most significant Minoan palace towns on Crete. If you visit *Knossós (see p. 82)* first, you'll have a better idea of what Festós looked like 3,500 years ago – today all that remains are a few foundation walls. However, the setting is delightful, on a hilly plateau with views of the Psilorítis and Asteroúsia mountains. If you want to

INSIDER TIP
Fabulous views

save the admission fee, just go to the terrace of the excavation café, probably the loveliest on the island, plus you'll have close views of the Minoan town. If you are genuinely interested in Minoan Crete, then drive another 2 km to the excavation of the tiny Minoan palace at *Agía Triáda (April–Oct daily from 9.30 am–4.30 pm,*

otherwise *Tue-Sun 9 am–3 pm | admission 4 euros)* in a shady little wood. *April–Oct daily from 8 am–8 pm, otherwise daily from 8 am–5 pm | admission 8 euros | K6*

10 MÍRES

13 km / 20 mins from Mátala by car

INSIDER TIP
A must-see for market lovers

On Saturday mornings, this is where the region's farmers meet and take up (temporary) residence in the *kafenía* and fast-food restaurants, dine on souvláki and drink *rakí*. Street sellers have pomegranate juice and nuts for visitors, and the stalls sell all sorts of items ranging from imports from China to oil and fruits of the region – anything and everything that will make a little money. *L6*

11 VÓRI

14 km / 15 mins from Mátala by car

Traditional costumes and weapons, crafts, agricultural and kitchen equipment from the last 200 years are beautifully arranged here in cabinets labelled with exacting accuracy. *Vóris Museum of Ethnology (April–Oct daily from 11 am–5 pm | admission 3 euros) K6*

12 GÓRTIS

19 km / 25 mins from Mátala by car

The ruins of the island's Roman capital are on both sides of the road. On the north, they are fenced in and you have to pay to get in *(April–Oct daily from 8 am–8 pm, otherwise 8 am–3 pm | admission 6 euros)*. See the remains of the towering walls of the *Títus*

In Míres market local people come to shop and chat

Basilica, which dates back to the sixth century BCE, and the *Odéon*, a small Roman theatre for music and pantomime. Now under cover and behind bars are 12 of what were once 20 tablets of rules, carved around 500 BCE. You'll learn a lot about the civil and criminal law of the time from these 42 stone blocks with 17,000 letters. Behind them is a meadow with an ancient olive tree, under which Zeus, the father of the gods, allegedly fathered Minos with Europa.

On the other side of the road (no admission) 🐷 are remains of countless Roman buildings, including an amphitheatre, the Governor's palace and a thermal spa. Very few visitors, so you can enjoy antiquity in delightful peace and solitude. *Ⅲ L6*

🔟 ZARÓS

25 km / 40 mins from Mátala by car
This large town on the 340-m-high southern slope of the Ída Mountain is well known for its trout farming and its many beautiful hiking possibilities. Two good trout tavernas (€€) are situated on the road to the little mountain lake of Záros. *Ⅲ L6*

ÁGIOS NIKÓLAOS & AROUND

PICTURESQUE RESORT & GREAT OUTINGS

Shabby chic not your thing? Then Mirabéllo Bay should be the perfect holiday region for you. Even the Venetians once called it a "lovely sight". Everything here is beautifully looked after and spotlessly clean. Crete's tourism began here in the early 1970s: Walt Disney, Jules Dassin and Mélina Merkoúri were among the first guests in the beautiful bay.

Countless other hotels have been added to the early luxury establishments on the outskirts of Ágios Nikólaos, at Ístro and Eloúnda,

In the evening, when the lights come on, everybody is drawn to the tavernas at Lake Límni

where celebrities from all over the world like to come on holiday and even play golf.

Completely normal Crete awaits you in the hilly hinterland. There, you will encounter flocks of sheep and goats on the road, see the older generation sitting in the old-fashioned *kafenía*, as they have always done. On the Lassíthi Plateau, a mule might carry you up to the cave where the little-visited excavation sites of Lató and Goúrnia tell you about Crete's long history.

ÁGIOS NIKÓLAOS & AROUND

★ **SPINALÓNGA**
A lepers' village built within the walls of a Venetian fortress ➤ p. 99

Λιμένας Χερσονήσου
Limenas Chersonisou

Αγία Βαρβάρα
Agia Varvara

6 Sisi

Μίλατος
Milatos

Σταλίδα
Stalida

Μάλια
Malia

90

Μοχός
Mochos

Νεά
Νε

Αβδού
Avdou

Κράσι
Krasidi

29 km, 35 mins

Γωνιές
Gonies

Άνω Κερά
Ano Kera

Τζερμιάδο
Tzermiado

Κάτω Μετόχι
Kato Metochi

Λαγού
Lagou

Μέσα Λασίθι
Mesa Lasithi

7 Lassíthi Plateau ★

Πλάτη
Plati

Άγιος Γεώργιος
Agios Georgios

Ψυχρό
Psychro

Καμινάκι
Kaminaki

Γαννιτσι
Gannitsi

45 km, 60 n

Μάλ
Male

Χριστός
Christos

▲
N

4 km
2.49 mi

MARCO POLO HIGHLIGHTS

★ LASSÍTHI PLATEAU
A fertile mountain oasis with ancient caves, beautiful villages and a folk museum ➤ p. 101

★ GOÚRNIA
See how the Minoans lived: the ruins of a 3,500-year-old city, open to all citizens ➤ p. 103

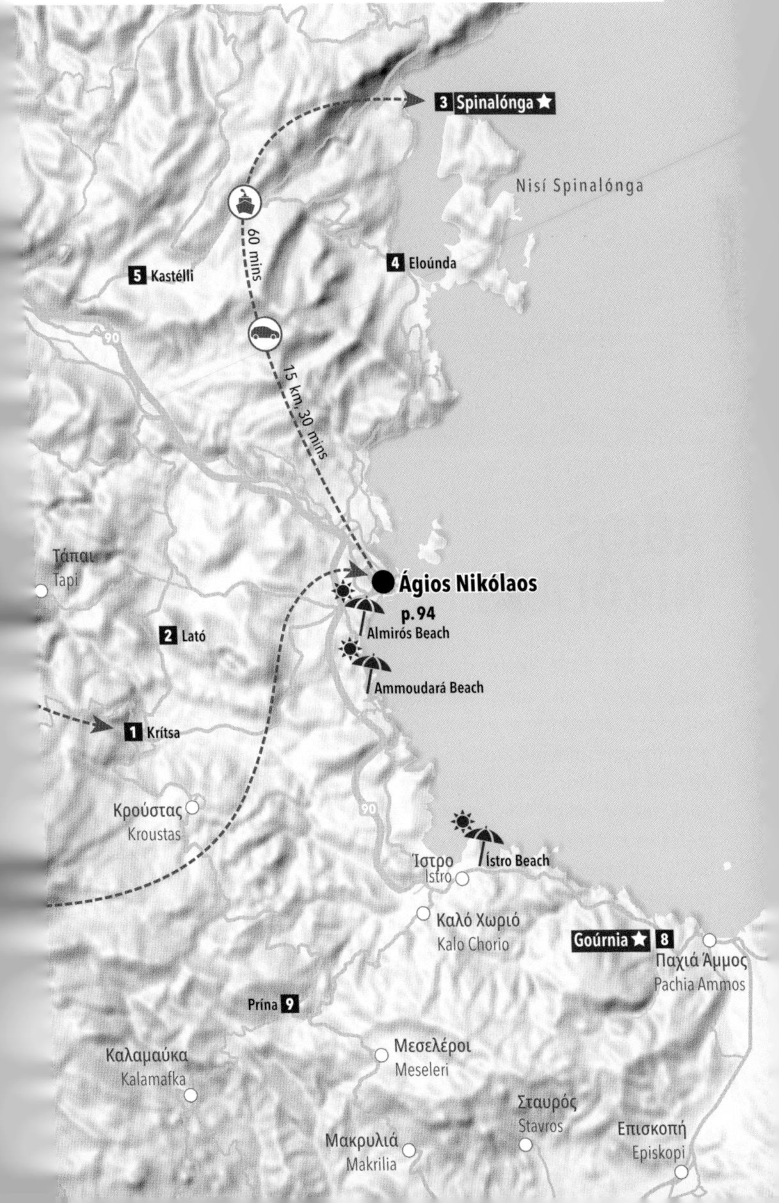

3 Spinalónga ★
Nisí Spinalónga
60 mins
4 Eloúnda
5 Kastélli
90
15 km, 30 mins
Τάπαι
Tapí
Ágios Nikólaos
p. 94
Almirós Beach
2 Lató
Ammoudará Beach
1 Krítsa
Κρούστας
Kroustas
90
Ίστρο
Istro
Ístro Beach
Καλό Χωριό
Kalo Chorio
Goúrnia ★ 8
Παχιά Άμμος
Pachia Ammos
Prína 9
Μεσελέροι
Meseleri
Καλαμαύκα
Kalamafka
Σταυρός
Stavros
Επισκοπή
Episkopi
Μακρυλιά
Makrilia

Agía Triáda Church: the contemporary mosaic above the portal is in classic Byzantine style

ÁGIOS NIKÓLAOS

(□ R5) **The little town that the locals simply call "Ágios" for short manages something of a balancing act: despite having more than 20,000 beds for visitors, even at peak season Ágios Nikólaos never feels like an overrun tourist spot. As the administrative capital for eastern Crete, it is extremely independent and, unlike Iráklio, Chaniá and Réthimno, doesn't have an urban atmosphere.**

The cafés on the shore of the small inland lake are only one centre; the streams of tourists are also drawn to the many cafés along the long coastal road that surrounds an entire rocky peninsula, as well as to the harbour front and the inviting shops in the pedestrian zone. Ágios (pop. 27,000) has developed organically, if haphazardly and not always imaginatively. The town is at its most beautiful on the shore of the small lake, *Límni Vulisméni*, which since 1870 has been connected to the town's harbour by a channel.

You'll see fishing boats bobbing on the lake, which is surrounded by rocky cliffs on two sides. Here you will also find tables and chairs set out by taverna and café owners. Just as nice are the cafés up at the cliff top, where you have a view of the lake and the harbour. At night, the eastern side is the busiest.

SIGHTSEEING

AGÍA TRIÁDA CHURCH

Are these angels vegetarians? Possibly. The tiny carrot in the modern mosaics above the portal to the main church could be a reference to the eating habits of the three little angels that Abraham and his wife Sarah are looking after. Or, on the other hand, to a preference of the mosaic artist.

The many large-scale murals inside the church tell other biblical stories, with more details for you to decode. If you know a little bit about the Bible, you'll have a wonderful time here. Unlike most medieval murals, these new frescoes in the traditional Byzantine style are easy to decipher. *Mostly 7 am–noon and 4–7.30 pm | admission free | ⏱ 15–30 mins*

ARCHAEOLOGICAL MUSEUM

Life was uncertain in ancient times. People could never be sure that the world would still be all right a year later, or that the soil would bring forth food for them. That was why they honoured fertility goddesses. And they imagined them to be like the goddess Mírtos, who can be seen in the Archaeological Museum. Her insignificant head sits on a long, phallic neck. She has two prominent breasts and a (painted) triangle for her pubic area, while her spindly arms fade into insignificance. Also interesting is a clay house model illustrating how people lived here around 3,250 years ago. The fact that they believed in life after death is confirmed by a very special skull from the first century. It is displayed here as it was found: surrounded by a wreath of thin golden leaves and with a coin in the mouth. The deceased needed this to pay Charon, the ferryman on the river to the kingdom of the dead. *Tue–Sun 8 am–3 pm | admission 6 euros | Odós Paleológu 68 | ⏱ 25–40 mins*

EATING & DRINKING

ÍTANOS

Although sitting here is nicer in the evenings, this unpretentious taverna is perfect for a quick, very good lunch with the locals. It is in a central location, close to the town's main square. The Cretan dishes are freshly prepared every day, and are presented appetisingly in heated containers. You'll only need the menu to find out the prices. The menu will depend largely on the season, and it's excellent value for money. *Daily 11 am–11 pm | Odós Kípru 1 | €*

MIGÓMIS

Romantics will love this taverna high above the sea: every evening, a skilled pianist provides the musical entertainment. Half the tables on the open veranda are elegantly laid, the other half are for guests who only want a drink. The menu is international, and includes duck breast and salmon. *Daily from 11 am | Odós Nikolaou Plastíra 20 | migomis.gr | €€€*

PÉLAGOS

The traditional *kaiki* (fishing boat) on the terrace of this classic villa indicates what is best here: fresh fish. You can enjoy it in what is probably the prettiest taverna garden in the town. The furnishings are colourful, while the grilled squid with honey and fennel is a tender treat. *Daily noon–midnight | Odós Stratigú Koráka 10 | €€€*

SHOPPING

BLANC DU NIL

You'll leave this boutique all in white (but not carrying a bouquet). Everything in it is white – cool white blouses, shirts, dresses and trousers. The only material is the finest quality Egyptian cotton. No wedding dresses, though. *Odós Sfakianáki 9*

KERÁ

Lovely shop with tastefully selected items (both new and old); woven articles, jewellery, marionettes and dolls from Greek workshops. *Odós J. Kundurú 8 | at the harbour underneath the restaurant Cretan Stars*

MARKET

A large weekly market takes place every Wednesday morning on *Odós Ethnikís Antistáseo*, which starts on the lakeshore.

SPORT & ACTIVITIES

The town itself offers little in terms of water sports, which is why sporty types go to Pláka, 16 km to the north. Here, *Plaka Water Sports (in front of Hotel Blue Palace | tel. 69 47 69 75 99 | plaka-watersports.gr)* offer water-skiing, wakeboarding, canoes and pedalos.

You can also hire jet skis and a 25hp motor boat to sail on your own, without a boating licence, provided you pass a brief training session.

INSIDER TIP

Become you own skipper

Fresh from the boat: *Pélagos* restaurant presents the fish on offer in a picturesque *kaiki*

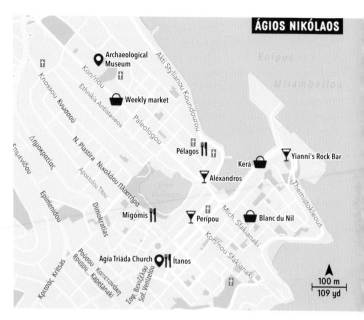

ÁGIOS NIKÓLAOS

Archaeological Museum
Weekly market
Pélagos
Kerá
Yianni's Rock Bar
Aléxandros
Migómis
Peripou
Blanc du Nil
Agía Triáda Church
Ítanos

100 m
109 yd

WELLNESS

For a perfect day of relaxation, drive the 12 km to Eloúnda. Here you can visit numerous luxury hotels with generously designed, expensive spas which are open to non-residents, provided that you book in advance. The spa in the *Blue Palace Resort (tel. 28 41 06 55 00 | bluepalace.gr)* is particularly beautiful.

BEACHES

The most beautiful beach in town is the almost 120-m-long pebble *Kitroplatía Beach*, about five minutes from the harbour. Along the coastal road to Eloúnda, on the edge of town, lies the sandy *Havanía Beach*. Almost 1.5 km southeast of the town, you will find the 250-m-long sandy *Almirós Beach*, and, about a mile further along the road to Sitía, lies the sandy 100-m-long *Ammoudará Beach*. An easy and cheap way of visiting the beaches of *Kaló Chorió* and *Ístro* further to the east is with the public bus service. Tavernas, deckchairs and umbrellas can be found on all of these beaches.

NIGHTLIFE

Mega discos are out; they no longer exist. In Ágios, people prefer to spend the nights in the many smaller bars along the road around the peninsula, between the harbour and Kitroplatía Beach. Plenty of dancing goes on, especially when parties are announced on the notice board and on Facebook.

ALÉXANDROS

Music bar in a roof garden with a view of the lake, lushly decorated with flowers. Dance music for every age and taste, which sometimes makes older guests look back on the stories of their lives nostalgically, as the DJ will play oldies on request. Drinks on offer include Spanish sangría and Greek champagne. *Daily from 8 pm | Odós Kondiláki 1*

PERÍPOU

This culture café high above the lake also sells CDs and books as well as being a sophisticated cultural stage.

Locals and tourists mingle from 10 pm with wine and cocktails. The music ranges from Greek songwriters to hard techno. *Daily from 10 pm | Odós 28is Octovríou 25*

INSIDER TIP Culture and cocktails

YIANNI'S ROCK BAR

Owner and DJ Yianni still plays his music on CDs. Let's rock! is his motto, and he's always happy to oblige with requests. Look beyond your immediate surroundings, and you'll see the sea. *Odós I. Kundúru 1*

No mercy: in the medieval fort of Spinalónga, lepers were left to fend for themselves

AROUND ÁGIOS NIKÓLAOS

1 KRÍTSA

9 km / 10 mins from Ágios Nikólaos by car

This lovely mountain village is sometimes completely overrun by visitors. It has plenty of souvenir shops, cafés and tavernas to cater for them, as well as a Byzantine art jewel at the bottom edge of the village right on the road from Ágios: the *Panagía i Será* church *(only April–Oct Tue–Sun 8.30 am–3 pm | admission 3 euros)*, with perfectly intact frescoes dating from the 15th to the 17th century. The dome in the nave does not show Christ as the ruler of all; instead, there are four scenes from the New Testament: Mary in the temple; the baptism of Jesus; the resurrection of Lazarus; and Jesus's entrance into Jerusalem on Palm Sunday. In the centre of the dome, four angels represent heaven. The prophets of the Old Testament that prophesised the coming of Christ are depicted on the lower edge. The pendentives connecting the dome to the nave show, as is often the case, the apostles Matthew, Mark, Luke and John, whose gospels spread the teachings of Jesus to the people. Even for those not interested in theology, the images of hell on the west wall will leave a strong impression. *Q5*

2 LATÓ

13 km / 20 mins from Ágios Nikólaos by car

Once upon a time, princes had ruins built in their parks because it looked so romantic. However, on the green hill of Lató, history really was the architect. A small theatre, the foundations of an old temple, the tiny, antique market square, a cistern, the ruins of old houses and the town wall are all that is left of the town that thrived here between the seventh and fourth centuries BCE. Today they are the perfect spot for a picnic. *April–Oct, Tue–Sun 8.30 am–3 pm | admission 3 euros | Q5*

3 SPINALÓNGA ★

1 hr from Ágios Nikólaos by boat or 25 mins from Eloúnda by boat

The Venetian fortress island Spinalónga *(Kalidón)* launched its tourist career as the "Island of Lepers": between 1913 and 1957, it was a leper colony. The afflicted lived among the medieval walls in total isolation in a village they built themselves; they were also buried here. Amongst the lepers were craftsmen and farmers, a hairdresser and even a priest; people married and had children. But healthy newborn babies were immediately taken from their mothers and sent to an orphanage in Crete. Apart from the sporadic visits of a doctor, the lepers had no medical care at all.

The road around the island is only about 1 km long. The trip out by excursion boat is worthwhile not only to experience a slight shiver while visiting the island, but also because of the diverse coastal scenery. A tour with an English guide is recommended; the guides bring the past to life with their retelling of the island's gruesome history.

INSIDER TIP
Guided tours

Daily boats from Ágios (12–17 euros), Eloúnda (10 euros) and Pláka (8 euros) | admission 8 euros, guided tour 2 euros | 🕮 R4

4 ELOÚNDA

12 km / 20 mins from Ágios Nikólaos by car

Blue-bloods and celebrities from all over the world often only know one place on Crete: unassuming Eloúnda. Leonardo di Caprio and Lady Gaga are only two of the big names that have holidayed here. Nowhere else on Crete will you find so many luxurious hotels of the highest (price) ratings so close together. Private pools and butler service are as much a matter of course as helicopter transfers and luxury yachts for day trips. But you wouldn't think it from looking at the place. The luxury hotels are unobtrusive, away from the village, and the better-known hotel guests prefer to remain anonymous in their cages. If you'd still like to see them, are not staying in the same hotel but are willing to spend a lot of money, then book a table in one of the hotel restaurants such as Peruvian-Japanese *Mistura* (tel. 28 41 06 70 00 | *eloundabeach. gr* | €€€) at the hotel *Eloúnda Beach*. Ordinary citizens appreciate the 400-m promenade, flanked by tavernas, from the tiny harbour to the dam on the large island of *Spinalónga* (not the same as the leper colony), which passes through former

Turn away from the beach for once and visit the rural Lassíthi Plateau

saltworks. In the flat waters, snorkellers can explore the remains of the ancient town of *Oloús*, of which there remains an early Christian floor mosaic right behind the *Canal Bar*. 🕮 R4

5 KASTÉLLI & AROUND

20 km / 30 mins from Ágios Nikólaos by car

With its old Venetian mansions and artfully wrought gates and railings, this very quiet village is one of the most beautiful in the region. Its narrow streets are full of wild geraniums. An alley lined with eucalyptus trees leads you into the neighbouring village of *Fourní*, where almond trees blossom at the end of March. Here at the village square María Sfiráki awaits you in her tavern *@Plátanos (daily from 8 am | €)* underneath an old plane tree, where she serves fresh salads and affordable dishes like rabbit or lamb's liver.

A track leads to the excavations of the Dorian city of *Dríros*, where the remains of an Apollo temple, cistern, altar and the Agorá can still be seen. *Admission free.* 🕮 Q4

6 SÍSI

22 km / 25 mins from Ágios Nikólaos by car

A pinch of Figuera on Mallorca, a touch of Norway and a generous dash of Crete – Sísi is an exceptional place. The centre is a mini fjord, where you can swim among the fishing boats. Palms reach up into the sky on the western shore, while on the other side people enjoy a glass or cup of something on the terraces of the cafés and bars. At the western exit to the fjord is a small sandy beach, and to the east there are a few fish tavernas on the quay. Hosts Níkos and Michális at *Angístri (daily from 11 am | €€)* are delightful. If you're not too bothered about the fjord, walk 1–2 km miles east, where there are more sandy/ shingle beaches. 🕮 P4

7 LASSÍTHI PLATEAU ⭐

45 km / 1 hr from Ágios Nikólaos by car

A day away from the sea can also be pleasant. Perhaps you'll find it so appealing that you'll make the spontaneous decision to spend a night in pure rural paradise on Crete's biggest high plain. It's certainly possible. From *Stalída (🕮 P4)* on the coastal motorway, an excellent road winds up in

generous bends to the foothills of the Díkti Mountains. A look back at the coast will amaze you: how delightfully small are even the big Cretan tourist centres Chersónisos and Mália, when compared with those on Spanish or Turkish coasts! The first mountain village, *Mochós*, welcomes you with one of the prettiest village squares on Crete – and it's time for your first coffee. In *Krasí* you'll see the island's oldest plane tree on the square with the large Venetian fountain. At the *Kerá Kardiótissa Monastery (daily from 8 am–6 pm | admission 2 euros)* you'll admire the icon of the Blessed Virgin Mary – a keen traveller: according to the legend, she was taken to Istanbul by Turks no fewer than three times, but every time she made it back home by herself. On her last flight, she allegedly brought not only the chain, but also the pillar that the Turks had chained her to. These can also be seen in the monastery: the chain on the icon in the church, and the pillar in the cloisters. Then comes the *Museum of Mankind (daily from 9 am–6 pm | admission 4 euros)*. A former customs officer tells you, in a charmingly naïve way, how he imagines the development of mankind from the earliest Stone Age to the moon landing.

At lunchtime, you'll be at the top of the *Ámbelos Afín (Ⅲ P5)* pass, where the eponymous restaurant *(daily from 11.30 am | €€)* has a delicious pork roast waiting for you. It is served with potatoes from the Lassíthi high plain. This plateau, which is surrounded by high

INSIDER TIP
Hog roast

mountains, is 10 km long and 5 km wide. More than 20 villages are arranged around the perimeter to waste as little as possible of the fertile soil.

The drive from the top of the pass to the 800-m plain takes only three minutes, and you'll be greeted by a few fabric-covered wind turbines. You can see them in old photos in all the tavernas up here: until well into the 1970s, there were thousands of these wind turbines on the Lassíthi Plateau, where they were used to draw up the groundwater. Now they have almost all been replaced by motor-driven pumps. The main destination for the many tourist buses up here is the *Diktéon Ándron stalactite cave (daily 9 am–3 pm, May–Sept sometimes until 7 pm | admission 4 euros)* above the village of *Psychró (Ⅲ P5)*. This was a place of worship from as early as the second millenium BCE. According to legend, it was here that Zeus was brought up by goats because his mother, Rhea, feared that his father, Kronos, would see him as a rival and devour him as he had Zeus's siblings. It is possible to ride up to the cave on mules. The cave is well lit and sturdy footwear is recommended.

However, as an individual traveller, Lassíthi has so much more to offer you. You can stroll through the peaceful, largely unspoilt villages, enjoy short walks around the fields, and just experience the pure rusticity. In the large village of *Ágios Geórgios* there is an interesting folk museum with an adjacent gallery *(daily 10 am–4 pm | admission 3 euros)*. The *Taverna Villaéti (daily from noon | €€)* on the

According to legend, baby Zeus was nursed by goats in the Diktéon Ándron stalactite cave

main road in the neighbouring village of Ágios Konstantínos serves various Lassíthian specialities and the proprietor's sister is one of the pioneers of the organic potato cultivation on the plateau. *P5*

8 GOÚRNIA ★

19 km / 25 mins from Ágios Nikólaos by car

On the coastal road on a low hill above the Gulf of Mirabéllo are the excavations of the Minoan city of Goúrnia. The foundation walls of the 3,500-year-old houses are in good condition and parts of the stairways that led to the upper floor can still be seen. Narrow, paved alleys lead to the former palace on the top of the hill. *Tue–Sun 8.30 am–3 pm | admission 4 euros | R6*

9 PRÍNA

19 km / 30 mins from Ágios Nikólaos by car

INSIDER TIP
A musical bonus

Would you like a private concert? Then make sure your MARCO POLO guide is clearly visible on your table at the taverna *Pitópoulis (daily from 11 am | €),* because host Dímitris is a well-known *lýra* player. Once a week (usually on Wednesday), he spends a whole evening playing for locals and other guests – and he'll be pleased to play you a few notes from his repertoire, provided his wife Stélla is happy on her own in the kitchen. Food and music are well matched: both are authentically Cretan. *Q6*

IERÁPETRA & AROUND

A TOUCH OF AFRICA

Arabic music mixes with Cretan sounds on the radio. Winds from the south blow in dust from the Sahara. In the centre of old town Ierápetra, a minaret towers upwards. There are hints of northern Africa everywhere in the landscape.

Ierápetra and its surroundings are an unusual part of Crete, completely different from the other parts of the island. Ierápetra can suffer from excessive heat in the summer, but it is an ideal holiday destination during the spring, autumn and winter. You can swim in

Apart from fabulous sandy beaches and turquoise sea, Chrísi has nothing else to offer – how relaxing!

the Libyan Sea even during December and January.

The only area well developed for tourism is between Mírtos and Makrigialós; the remaining coastal resorts are far from the main roads and are sought out by independent tourists. Beach idylls are provided by the islands of Chrísí and Koufonísi off the south coast, which attract excursion boats in summer. Both are uninhabited; they have the finest sandy beaches and no hotels at all.

IERÁPETRA & AROUND

MARCO POLO HIGHLIGHTS

★ **CHRISÍ ISLAND**
Have a Robinson Crusoe experience on this dreamy, uninhabited island
➤ p. 110

Nisí Día

Αγία Πελαγία
Agia Pelagia

Αχλάδα
Achlada

Παλαιόκαστρο
Paliokastro

Ηράκλειο
Iráklio

Γούρνες
Gournes

Λιμένας Χερσονήσου
Limenas Chersonisou

Δαμάστα
Damasta

Γάζι
Gázi

Καρτερός
Karteros

Κνωσσός
Knossos

Χερσόνησος
Hersonissos

Μάλι
Malia

Γωνιές
Goniés

Τύλισσος
Tilissos

Αρχάνες
Archanes

Καστέλι
Kasteli

Μοχός
Mochos

Τζερμι
Tzermi

Κάτω Ασίτες
Kato Asites

Δαφνές
Daphnes

Θραψανό
Thrapsano

Μαθιά
Mathia

Α
Ag

Παρθένι
Partheni

Ζαρός
Zaros

Αγία Βαρβάρα
Agia Varvara

Αρκαλοχώρι
Arkalohori

CRETE
ΚΡΗΤΗ

Άγιοι Δέκα
Agii Deka

Λιγόρτυνος
Ligortinos

Γαρίπα
Garipa

Ασήμι
Asimi

Άνω Βιάννος
Ano Viannos

Δεμάτι
Demati

Στέρνες
Sternes

Πύργος
Pyrgos

Καστρί
Kastri

Άρβη
Arvi

Άγιος Κύριλλος
Agios Kyrillos

9 Léndas ★
Dískos Beach

135 km, 2½ hrs

L i v i k ó

▲
10 km
6.21 mi

Μίλατος
Milatos

Nisí Spinalónga

Νεάπολη
Neápoli

Ελούντα
Eloúnta

Σητεία
Sitia

Σκοπή
Skopi

Άγιος Νικόλαος
Agios Nikolaos

Τουρλωτή
Tourloti

...ιγος
...ios

Κριτσά
Kritsa

Πισκοκέφαλο
Piskokefalo

Σκορδίλο
Skordilo

Καλό Χωριό
Kalo Chorio

Παχιά Άμμος
Pachia Ammos

7km, 2 hrs

Σταυροχώρι
Stavrochóri

Λιθίνες
Litines

5 Péfki

Ζήρος
Ziros

40 km, 50 mins

Θοι
ιτti

Βramianá
reservoir 7

Dasaki Butterfly Gorge 2

Κουτσουράς
Koutsouras

3 Makrigialos

6 Kapsá Monastery ★

8 Mírtos

Γρα Λυγιά
Gra Lygia

East Beach
Ierápetra
p.108

Φέρμα
Ferma

Καλό Νερό
Kalo Nero

Koufonísi
Island 4

Nisí Koufonísi

1 Chrisí Island ★

Nisí Chrisí

Pélagos

Ierápetra's old town features a well house and a minaret in the quiet *platía*

IERÁPETRA

(📖 R6) **In the beauty pageant of Cretan towns, Ierápetra (pop. 27,600) is happy to come last. There are other interests here. All that counts is vegetable cultivation; beach tourism is a side-show.**

Back in 1965, Paul Cooper from Holland introduced the farmers to the cultivation of cucumbers and tomatoes in greenhouses. Local farmers became the richest in the whole of Greece. For a time, there was also talk of building a private airport to speed up the transport of Crete's early vegetables to European markets. Even today, the plastic-covered *thermokípia* reach as far

as the outskirts of the town, sparkling like a huge lake in the sunlight. Almost every vehicle in the little town is a pick-up, because being the shopping centre for the farmers is Ierápetra's main function.

SIGHTSEEING

OLD TOWN

Ierápetra is no Greek idyll. But at least there is a very quiet quarter, where the town's Turkish population lived until 1913. You can easily spend an hour strolling around there. Start at the western end of the beach promenade. There is a *tiny fortress (Tue-Sun 8 am-3 pm | admission free)* that was built by the Venetians in 1626 with views from the battlements of the old town and harbour. Then make your way to the minaret you just spotted. It belongs to a permanently locked *mosque* with a well house on its square that has been restored. Then stroll back to the beach promenade, where a discreet signpost next to the *Levante* taverna indicates the *Napoleon House*. You can't go inside, but do look at it from the outside. It is said that Napoleon spent a night here in 1798 prior to his foray into Egypt.

ARCHAEOLOGICAL MUSEUM

If you've succumbed to the Minos virus or make pottery yourself, then you'll enjoy visiting this little museum in what was once a Turkish school. It has two Minoan potter's wheels and a lovely Minoan sarcophagus with hunting scenes. The section with three Minoans in a cart that is being pulled by animals is very unusual. The cart is on spoked rather than disc wheels – and we're talking more than 3,300 years ago! *Tue–Sun 8 am–3 pm | admission 2 euros | Odós Ethnikís Antistáseos | close to the square in the new town |* ⏱ *10–20 mins*

EATING & DRINKING

I SKÉDIA

White taverna by the sea on the outskirts of the town in the direction of Sitía. Floating cloths and ships' ropes for decoration, bamboo for the roof. George and Helen keep their taverna open all year round, and many of the locals are regulars who appreciate the authentic Cretan cuisine and excellent

value for money. *Daily from 1 pm | east of the hotel Petra Mare | €–€€*

LEVANTE

When the lovely smell of freshly grilled fish streams out of the kitchen, it practically pulls the sun-worshippers on the beach outside this restaurant off their towels. Vegetarians will also find plenty to enjoy in the friendly, rather chic taverna. Host Níkos thinks his moussaká – fresh from the oven – is the best.

> **INSIDER TIP**
> Delicious moussaká

Daily from 11 am | Odós Stratigoú Samouíl 38 | levante-restaurant-fish-taverna.business.site | €

PÓRTEGO

Bar, café and restaurant in 100-year old buildings with small and atmospheric inner courtyards. This place mainly caters for groups of people who love the typical mesédes. *Daily from 7.30 pm | Odós N Foniadáki 8 | €€€*

> **INSIDER TIP**
> Lovely group venue

SHOPPING

MARKET (LAIKÍ AGORÁ)

How farmers shop: the Saturday market in the east of the town is not aimed at tourists. *Odós Psilináki*

SPORT & ACTIVITIES

Ierápetra Watersports (tel. 69 44 76 65 07 | FB: ierapetrawater sports), a water sports school on Ierápetra's beach by the big Petra Mare hotel, offers courses in windsurfing, water-skiing and sailing; canoes and paddle boats can also be hired and you can book diving courses here.

BEACHES

There is a short sand-and-gravel beach in front of the many tavernas between the harbour and fortress. Considerably longer is the 🏄 *East Beach* which begins at the Hotel Petra Mare and stretches for many miles to the east. Numerous other beaches, mainly to the east, can be accessed by regular bus services.

WELLNESS

The best wellness centre is *Kallísti Spa (Katharádes | tel. 28 42 02 57 11 | FB: ostria resort & spa)* in the Óstria resort 5 km to the east of the town by the beach. It is also open to non-hotel residents.

NIGHTLIFE

The cafés and bars along the beach promenade are at their liveliest before midnight. After midnight, revellers withdraw to the *Privilege (from 10 pm)*, where the DJ mostly plays Greek rock. Locals also like to drive into the villages in the evenings: music bars and nightclubs can be found mainly in the *Odós Kirvá* behind the beachfront promenade *(e.g. Seven, Saxo, Insomnia)*. 5 km inland in the village of *Vaínia* at the *Ouzeri Plátanos (closed Mon)* on the village square you can enjoy a simple table wine and Cretan *mesédes* under mulberry trees.

AROUND IERÁPETRA

1 CHRISÍ ISLAND ★

50 mins from Ierápetra by boat

It's not possible to have more sand. The island of Chrisí is perfect for a day in the sun. Besides a taverna, a beach bar and dunes above which the bizarre roots and branches of the 10-m-high prickly juniper trees tower, there are also long white sandy beaches. Excursion and taxi boats come here daily from Ierápetra during the summer. Staying overnight is prohibited, but many young Greeks do not adhere to this rule – probably because there is no police station. Nude bathing is as common as partying on the beach at night, although almost nobody takes the three-hour trekking route around the island which offers no shade along the way. *Q–R8*

2 DASAKI BUTTERFLY GORGE

20 km / 30 mins from Ierápetra by car

Feel like a spot of climbing and stream crossing? Your enjoyable endeavours will be rewarded by large numbers of butterflies and a few small waterfalls. You'll need good shoes, and a towel is useful in case you miss your footing. There's no destination; you just turn back when you feel like it: take a picnic with you. The walk starts at the car park 1 km to the west of the village of Koutsoúra (*Communal Park of Koutsoúra* or *Dasaki Butterfly Gorge* on the signs). You can walk the gorge between May and November. *S6*

Sail to Koufonísi to bathe in the sea and contemplate the beauty of nature

🔞 MAKRÍGIALOS

24 km (14.9 miles) / 35 mins from Ierápetra by car

The village street is superfluous if you holiday here. Just follow the miles-long 🏖 *Makrígialos Beach*, and eventually you'll end up at almost every taverna in the village and, above all, at the harbour, where the excursion boat leaves for Koufonísi. The beach is fringed by tamarisks that provide shade, and you'll be perfectly comfortable among the boats in the taverna *To Stéki tou Miná (Mina's Place) (daily from 9 am | €)*, which is also frequented by the fishermen. The only reason you'll have to go inland is to humour your inner passion for history. In the centre of Makrígialos, close to the village church, lie the foundations of an ancient Roman villa from the first century CE (with free access). Just outside the village in the direction of Ierápetra a brown road-sign shows the way to the remains of a late Minoan villa. 🗺 *S6*

🔞 KOUFONÍSI

50 mins from Makrígialos by boat

The ancient Romans bred purple snails on the island to produce a dye that they used to colour the emperor's robes. In those days, Koufonísi even had a small, ultra-rich town with its own theatre. Now, like every other ancient building, it is slowly sinking into the sand, which adds the perfect finishing touch to the island's charms. Apart from that, the only thing to do here is to swim off any of its 36 white beaches with extremely fine sand, and where the water shimmers in flat bays in every imaginable shade of blue and turquoise.

INSIDER TIP
Robinson Crusoe's desert island

Just 15 minutes from the mooring point, you'll be able to spend a few hours pretending you are Robinson Crusoe. In summer, the boat trips by *Cretan Daily Cruises* (cretandailycruises.com) to Koufonísi almost all leave from Makrígialos. ⊞ U7

5 PÉFKI
28 km / 40 mins from Ierápetra by car

You go to Péfki if you're staying close by or happen to be driving through. Why? For a pleasant visit to the excellent, cosy *kafenío Zur Weinstube (daily from 9 am | €)* in the village centre. At the front you sit under vine tendrils, at the back you have views of a gorge that goes into the sea. The hosts put *rakí*, wine, cheese and olive on the table, cook a hearty omelette, and in summer also serve a small selection of dishes of the day. Two hours spent here are pure perfection. ⊞ T6

6 KAPSÁ MONASTERY ★
46 km / 1 hr from Ierápetra by car

It's unusual to find monasteries right beside the sea. This one is in a particularly lovely spot: it was built in the 15th century, partly into a rock face. There are few visitors, and the peace is heavenly, including on the tiny shingle beach with old tamarisks just below the monastery. *Daily from 8 am–noon and 4–7 pm.* ⊞ T6

7 BRAMIANÁ RESERVOIR *5 km / 10 mins from Ierápetra by car*

Built in 1986, this reservoir at *Gra Ligiá* has a capacity of 16 million litres of water and is the second largest in Crete. It irrigates the many greenhouses in the region. During the winter it is a bird paradise attracting more than 200 species. These include spotted eagles, snake eagles, peregrine falcons, bitterns, herons, pink flamingos and ibis. You can hike around the whole reservoir and there are observation points for amateur ornithologists. ⊞ Q–R6

8 MÍRTOS
15 km / 20 mins from Ierápetra by car

It is said that the wind hardly ever blows in Mírtos. And the coarse sand on the long beach doesn't stick to the skin. It's impossible to get lost in this hamlet; you can't miss a thing on the short beach promenade. If you holiday here, it's because you want to swim, swim and swim some more – and not have to choose from too many cafés, bars and tavernas in the evenings. Still, should you fall victim to a yearning for activity, there are two archaeological sites that are within walking distance. Close to the village, on the hills of *Foúrnu Kórfi* and *Pírgos*, archaeologists have uncovered the remains of an early Minoan villa with about 90 rooms and a double storey building. Both sites are open to visitors and can be reached by following the brown signs on the coastal road from Ierápetra. It is only possible to get there on foot and both ascents

Having a good old chat in Mírtos

start directly at their respective sign-post. ▢ Q6–7

🔟 LÉNDAS ⭐

90 km / 2 hrs from Ierápetra by car

Avoiding mass tourism has always been the watchword for backpacking tourists. Yet they've been coming here themselves in droves for 50 years now, without ever noticing that they, too, have become a mass. Be that as it may, this very isolated little place on the south coast takes excellent care of its visitors, leaving many things as they have been for years. Today, though, guests no longer stay in the grandparents' emptied-out bedrooms or huts, but in modern guestrooms and studios; they still hold hands in the cosy

beach tavernas, swim naked on *Dískos Beach* and drink wine on terraces right over the water. History has even left a little bit of culture: on the outskirts of the village are the ruins of a *Roman shrine to Asclepius (Tue–Sun 9 am–3 pm | admission free)*, the god of medicine. This coastal village, which is popular among young independent travellers and campers only has a few houses and tavernas. The white-washed houses are surrounded by beautiful flower gardens and there is a short sand and pebble beach in front of the village. A 15 minute walk brings you to a sandy beach where nude bathing is common. ▢ L7

INSIDER TIP
Like Adam & Eve

SITÍA & AROUND

PALM TREES, LEMONS, RAISINS

East and west are more than just directions on Crete. They're world views. Both extremes of the island have their loyal fans. By far the majority prefers the west. The far east is extreme in a different way: no high mountains, but plenty of appealing, African-style landscapes, rich red soil, small canyons, stony plains and a few palm trees. The towns are insignificant and relatively new. What count are the quaint villages and often unusual beaches.

The palm grove beach of Vái sometimes becomes a victim of its own success

The region is still undiscovered by mass tourism. Only Sitía, which is the lively rural centre of the region, has a single hotel that is slightly larger. There are only a few beaches around here, but they are very long and, apart from Vái, always have lots of space. There are only a few important historical sites, and the Minoan palace of Káto Zákros sees more turtles than visitors. Like the other regions, the sound of the lýra can still be heard, especially at festivals, where the instrument lies ready for use in many a taverna.

SITÍA & AROUND

MARCO POLO HIGHLIGHTS

★ VÁI
Crete's famous palm grove beach. Very photogenic, but always crowded during peak season ➤ p. 122

★ KÁTO ZÁKROS
Between a beach and a rocky wilderness lies a Minoan palace worth seeing ➤ p. 123

★ XERÓKAMBOS
Hardly anyone has discovered these lovely beaches yet ➤ p. 123

Kritikó

Nisí Psíra

Faneroménis **11**
Monastery

75 km, 1¾ hrs

13 Móchlos

Μυρσίνη
Myrsini

12 Chamési

Κιμουριώτ
Kimouriot

Έξω Μουλιανά
Exo Mouliana

Παρασπόρι
Paraspori

Αχλαδία
Achladia

Σφάκα
Sfaka

Σκορδίλο
Skordilo

Λάστρος
Lastros

Άγιος Σπυρίδ
Agios Spir
Νέα **9**
Presós

Χρυσοπηγή
Chrisopigi

Κάτω Κρυά
Kato Kria

Συκιά
Sykia

CRETE

10 Thriptí

Ορεινό
Orino

Άγιος Στέφανος
Agios Stefanos

Λιθίνες
Litines

Σταυροχώρι
Stavrochori

Άγιος Ιωάννης
Agios Ioannis

Σχινοκάψαλα
Shinokapsala

Πιλαλήματα
Pilalimata

Φέρμα
Ferma

Γαλήνη
Galini

Μακρύ Γιαλός
Makrygialos

Μαύρος Κόλυμπος
Mavros Kolimbos

Καλό Νερό
Kalo Nero

Livikó

Nisí Dragonáda

Nisí Gianisáda

Pélagos

Nisí Elása

☀🏖 **3** Ítanos

🏖 **4** Vái ★

🚗 70 km, 80 mins

2 Tóplou Monastery

●Sitía
p. 118

1 Agía Fotiá

🚗

Palékastro **5**

☀🏖 Chióna Beach

10 km, 15 mins

σκοκέφαλο
kokefalo

○ Σταυρομένος
Stavromenos

○ Καρύδι
Karidi

○ Αδραβάστοι
Adravasti

○ Σίτανος
Sitanos

Ζάκρος
Zakros

ΚΡΗΤΗ

☀🏖 **6** Káto Zákros ★

andrás Plateau

○ Ζήρος
Ziros

οι
eni
○

έσα Απίδι
Mesa Apidi

☀🏖 **7** Xerókambos ★

Ξερόκαμπος
Xerokampos

ύδουρας
oudouras

Pélagos

▲
4 km
2.49mi

A shady place in the far east of Crete, a region that is perfect for independent travellers

SITÍA

(*T4*) **Sitía (pop. 18,300) could have been made for slowing down. It's unlikely that anyone here has ever experienced stress. A taverna's tables and chairs stand on the green strip of a four-lane highway – but the waiter is still the very picture of health.**

The town of Sitía starts directly at the east end of the beach promenade, where the cafés and restaurants draw all life to them. The shops that are important to the locals are all within a few metres of the beach *platía*; the alleys that lead up to the castle are all residential areas full of flowers and cats. Even the harbour of Sitía is quiet. There's a ferry twice a week, the occasional small freighter, and that's it.

SIGHTSEEING

ARCHAEOLOGICAL MUSEUM

Here's a young lad you should see! A Minoan carved him 3,500 years ago out of ivory from a hippopotamus. He chiselled his fine hair out of serpentinite stone, and originally his eyes were mountain crystals. His physical beauty was matched by golden magnificence: sandals, bangles, belt and loincloth were covered with gold leaf. You hardly notice that the pretty fellow is only 0.5 m tall. *Tue–Sun 8 am–3 pm | admission 3 euros | at the town exit on the road towards Ierápetra |* ⊙ *20–30 mins*

EATING & DRINKING

CRETAN HOUSE

Do you prefer to sit somewhere down

to earth and right by the water? Good run-of-the-mill Greek cuisine awaits you here – in large portions. The menu is extensive, and includes an excellent rabbit *stifádo* and a scampi gratin. There's often live Greek music on Saturdays. *Daily from 10 am | Odós Karamanlí 1 | €€*

MITSAKÁKIS

You'd better keep an eye on your calories in this confectionery which is the best in town. *Loukoumádes*, deep-fried pastries with honey and sesame are eaten both for breakfast and as a midnight snack, and the creamy custard pastry pie *galaktoboúreko* is a sweet dream. *Daily from 9 am–1 pm | Odós K. Karamanlí 5 | €*

@TO STÉKI

This taverna, which doesn't look like much, provides a fascinating experience as it is probably the only eatery in Europe where tables and chairs are on the central reservation of a four-lane road. The food is simple and excellent value for money and the experience is truly unique. *Daily from 11 am | Odós Papandréou 7 | €*

SHOPPING

MATTHAÍOS JEWELS

Matthaíos Karnakákis is from Sitía. He makes silver, gold and platinum jewellery that is inspired by Minoan and Byzantine originals. However, he also designs his own unique, often very playful modern line. The prices are extremely reasonable. *Odós Fountalídou 1 | FB: MttaiosJewels*

SITIAKÁ GLIKÁ ARÉTOUSA

Anna Garefaláki's ethnic grocery is a little shop that specialises in products from the region. It includes lots of sweet things, and also has *rakí*, wine and ouzo on the shelves. *Odós El. Venizélou/Odós Daskalogiánni*

SPORT & ACTIVITIES

The town of Sitía itself is not recommended as a holiday destination for sports enthusiasts. The next water sport centre is about 25 km away, in Vái.

BEACHES

The relatively stony town beach begins at the town's eastern edge. Long bathing days are better spent on the beaches of Vái and Káto Zákros which can be reached by regular bus services.

NIGHTLIFE

Ultra-cool parties often develop quite spontaneously in the little bars along the harbour. However, there's no room for big discos.

BLACK HOLE

Thanks to its excellent cocktails, the Black Hole (seating inside and out) is always the number one venue in town. Occasionally there is also live music. *Odós Karaveláki 7*

NOUVELLE BOUTIQUE

The audience is usually younger here than elsewhere and the music louder, thanks to the in-house DJ. *Odós El. Venizélou 161*

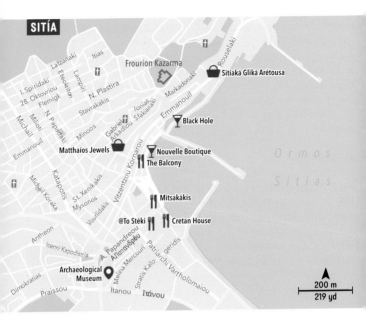

SITÍA

Frourion Kazarma

Sitiaká Gliká Arétousa

Black Hole

Matthaíos Jewels

Nouvelle Boutique
The Balcony

Mitsakákis

@To Stéki
Cretan House

Archaeological
Museum

Ormos Sitías

200 m
219 yd

AROUND SITÍA

1 AGÍA FOTIÁ

7 km / 10 mins from Sitía by car

If you're in the mood for a little archae-ological expedition, take the bus or a taxi to Agía Fotiá. In the fields below the village, archaeologists have exca-vated an early Minoan cemetery with a large number of shaft graves and tomb chambers. A brown sign saying *Archaeological Site* shows the way. Continue about 250 m on the dirt road until you reach the fenced-in excavation site on the low *Kouphóta hill* with ruins of an early Minoan set-tlement. As the beautifully prepared, EU-funded excavations are usually closed because of a shortage of attendants, you will have to look for a hole in the fence. Which isn't difficult: there are several of them. On the way back to Sitía there is a small, bleak peninsula behind an old olive oil factory with the remains of the set-tlement of Trypitós from Hellenic times. There are no attendants there, either. *U5*

INSIDER TIP
At your own risk

2 TÓPLOU MONASTERY

21 km / 30 mins from Sitía by car

The monastery's few monks recently sold large sections of this still com-pletely unspoilt northeastern part of the island to multinational investors, who have plans to build Crete's largest luxury resort there, including several golf courses. Conservationists took the matter to the Supreme Court of Justice, but the monastery won. The landscape here may be "developed". Construction work has not yet commenced, so seize this opportunity to experience northeast Crete while it is still "underdeveloped". The fortress-like medieval monastery is the only building for miles around, and is like an oasis in the midst of barren rocks and poor meadows. The *church* has one of Greece's loveliest icons, with numerous figures. It was painted by one Johannes Kornáros in 1770, and illustrates in many miniature-like individual representations the text of a seventh century ode entitled, "Thou art all-powerful, oh Lord!". Some people wish it would produce a miracle round about now. Surprisingly unspoilt and pleasantly original is the nameless *taverna (daily from 9 am–6 pm | €)* by the entrance to the monastery. The landlords are typically welcoming: when a couple enters, but only orders one portion, they are given two small plates and place settings anyway. Sometimes, the landlord feels a need to make sure that his guests respect the local eating habits: if he finds that you only have chicken on your fork, and no beans, he is going to intervene! *Daily 9 am–1 pm and 2–6 pm | admission 3 euros.* ⌕ U5

3 ÍTANOS

25 km / 40 mins from Sitía by car

Bathing on the edge of the desert – that's what an hour on the beach at Ítanos feels like. Simple houses rise from the dunes. A signpost in the middle of nowhere names the hamlet as Erimoúpoli, which means "Town of Solitude". Even the sparse remains of an ancient town with two early Christian basilicas are scattered around it. From the sandy beach with its crystal-clear waters, the view stretches as far as Cape Síderos, the northeastern tip of Crete, which the military has unfortunately claimed for itself. Ítanos is a perfect alternative to the crowded, palm tree-lined beach of Vái which is close by. There are no buses getting you here, no deckchairs on the beach and not a single hotel in sight for miles. ⌕ U4

INSIDER TIP
Truly wild & remote

Tóplou Monastery has a strict dress code: no shorts, and shoulders must be covered

🔹 VÁI ★ 🐜

25 km / 35 mins from Sitía by car

Of all the beaches on Crete, the one at Vái is the most overrated. The fine sand beach adjoins Crete's biggest palm tree grove, although no one is allowed to go there. It became world-famous when it was still unfenced because many hippies preferred to camp here rather than be conscripted to fight in Vietnam. Every day during the summer, Vái now attracts more visitors than it can handle. The beach car park has become bigger than the beach itself. There are no hotels yet, but there are two *tavernas (daily from 9 am | €)*, both of which belong – yes, you've guessed it – to Tóplou Monastery. The water-sports station also has to lease it premises from the monks. But decide for yourself. If you find it all too awful for words, it won't take you long to get to the empty beaches like the ones at Ítanos, Palékastro and Káto Zákros.
🗺 *U–V4*

🔹 PALÉKASTRO

24 km / 35 mins from Sitía by car

The large inland village of Palékastro has been lucky. It is so far from the airport at Iráklio that the major international organisers are not interested in it because of the long transfer times – although it has some wonderful beaches. This means that it attracts independent travellers. It's easy to get to the main beaches at Maridáki, Koureménos and Chióna, which are about 2–3 km from the village square, on foot or by moped. There are several tiny bays to the south of 🐜 *Chióna Beach* which are mainly nudist. Wind- and kitesurfers from all over the world

Land of quiet olive groves: the countryside around Sitía

meet on *Kouréménos Beach*. The beach at Chióna has various excavations of a *Minoan town (Tue–Sun 8 am–3 pm | admission 2 euros)* and three excellent tavernas. You will struggle to find a more idyllic setting on Crete than that provided by the two taverns located at the northern end of the beach. *Chióna (daily from noon | €€€)* and *Bátis (daily from noon | €€€)* both have terraces looking out over the sea towards the Middle East.

Sandwiched between the village and beach, you will find Olga in her tavern *Kakaviá (daily from 10 am | €€)* who has been serving mainly Cretan guests for over 50 years with her fish soup according to an ancient secret recipe given to her by a fisherman. At the *platía* of Palékastro visit the restaurant *Hellas (daily from 8 am | €)* which is traditional and unpretentious. At night it is the meeting place for locals and tourists alike. 📖 *U5*

6 KÁTO ZÁKROS ★ ☀

45 km / 1 hr from Sitía by car

It's a promise: it's going to be an entertaining day! If you're bathing on the miles-long shingle beach at Káto Zákros, remember there isn't a single piece of land between you and the coasts of Israel and Palestine, about 850 km away. That's vast. Káto Zákros itself consists of just a few little houses, loosely scattered over the coastal plain. It's hard to imagine anything more isolated. Just ten minutes away, giant turtles sun themselves among the ruins of the 3,500-year-old walls of a *Minoan palace town (April–Oct daily from 8 am–6 pm, Nov–March Tue–Sun 8 am–3 pm | admission 6 euros)* that once had 300 rooms – the eastern-most one on Crete. From here, the Minoans travelled across the sea and traded with Egypt and other empires in the Middle East. They also had a copper-smelting furnace in Káto Zákros, the remains of which can still be seen here as one of the oldest industrial monuments in Europe. They were bold.

But you don't really have to be bold today to enter the *Valley of the Dead*. Close to the palace, the path leads past a stream and up into the mountain village of *Zákros*, just a two-hour walk away. The first one-third of the path is the loveliest. You walk through a forest of oleanders that are taller than a man, and can see the numerous grottoes and caves in the reddish rock faces where the Minoans and early Christians once buried their dead. But Káto Zákros also offers modern art: the owner of the *Terra Minoica* apartments on the road just above the beach displays his interesting figures made of recycled metal and scrap. The taverna *Platanákis (daily from 10 am | €)*, located on the road next to the harbour, serves particularly good food with a twist on the traditional Cretan cuisine. 📖 *V6*

7 XERÓKAMBOS ★ ☀

43 km / 70 mins from Sitía by car

Despite having been accessible by tarmac roads for years, Xerókambos, in the very south-east of the island, is still a secret hideaway for people who prefer quiet beaches. There are many of them here: small hidden bays in the east and the 500-m-long, wide sandy *Ámbelos Beach* on the south coast. An unusual sight is sandy *Árgylos Beach* with its cliffs of pure clay. There are a few isolated tavernas and guesthouses and a few umbrellas to rent. Between the beaches archaeologists have uncovered the ruins of a Hellenic settlement on a plateau next to a St Nicholas chapel. 🕮 *U6*

◳ CHANDRÁS PLATEAU

31 km / 40 mins from Sitía by car

The main reason for driving up to the Chandrás Plateau is a longing for a rural idyll. All around the village of Chandrás farmers grow quince and giant pumpkin. Energy is produced here with 18 wind turbines and many small solar farms. In August and September, grapes are spread in the

Dolce vita on Crete: eat and drink in the shade by Káto Zákros Beach

village lanes so that they dry into sultanas. Magical all year round is the enchanted and tiny hamlet of Voíla near Chandrás. Now deserted, it was once home to a Venetian noble family who eventually converted to Islam. In the chapel, which is always open (turn the key to the right to enter), you find a mural showing the Virgin Mary with the baby Jesus above a tomb, and the local family in their traditional dress from the 16th century at her feet. The identity of the deceased is shown in a small mural: it is a young girl on her deathbed. The entire scene is rather touching. If you feel hungry in Chandrás, there are two simple *tavernas* (€) in the village square. ☐ T–U6

9 NÉA PRESÓS

16 km / 35 mins from Sitía by car

If you ever want to be all alone in an ancient town, climb up the hill that once bore the ancient Présos. A few sheep and goats will keep you company, but travel groups or attendants are nowhere to be seen. Nor is there much that is ancient, either, even though the hill was inhabited for 1,500 years during the entire period of Greco-Roman antiquity. What remains are the foundations of a temple, a house and a few stone blocks scattered about. But what sticks in your mind is the memory of a remote spot in the mountains, of pure nature. *Freely accessible | access road 2 km, well signposted in the village of Néa Présos.* *T6*

10 THRIPTÍ

50 km / 90 mins from Káto Chorió by car

Vines are cultivated here just below the 1,476 m high *Afendís Kawússi,* in a landscape which is reminiscent of the tea plantations in the Indian and Sri Lankan highlands. Vintners live here from summer until autumn and here you'll see a very ancient side of Crete. You can reach Thriptí by jeep via a forest road from *Káto Chorió.* From here you can drive across the mountains to *Orinó,* with its many threshing floors and carob trees, through untouched mountain villages like *Skinokápsala* and *Ágios Jánnis,* to reach the southern coast at *Koutsounári.* *S6*

11 FANEROMÉNIS MONASTERY

10 km / 15 mins from Sitía by car

Fancy something unusual, but somehow typically Cretan? Then leave Sitía on the road to Iráklio, and after 2 km turn right onto a narrow road signposted "Agion Panton Gorge". The road ends after about 10 km at a small village that is inhabited in summer only for the wine harvest, and in winter for the olive harvest. However, the *taverna (€)* is usually open all year round – and usually without guests. The landlady is delighted whenever a guest does turn up and she always has supplies of fresh salad ingredients and vegetables. Just 50 steps from this unusual spot is a no less curious, long-since abandoned, small *monastery.* Probably founded in the 15th century, it is boldly positioned over the gorge. You can see a few remains of 17th-century frescoes in the sooty vaults of the church. Somehow, it goes perfectly with the general ghost-town atmosphere that prevails. *T5*

12 CHAMÉSI

10 km / 15 mins from Sitía by car

A spot for all those who love the beauty of simplicity: on a hilltop southeast of this traditional mountain village are the foundation walls of the only oval-shaped *estate (admission free)* from Minoan times. You can enjoy a magnificent view across the land and sea from a field full of fennel, aromatic thyme, sage and oregano. To get there from the western end of the village, turn left beneath the remains of two windmills onto a dirt track that ends at the excavation site after about 700 m. *T5*

🔟 MÓCHLOS

30 km / 45 mins from Sitía by car

You don't get to Móchlos by chance. There's nothing, absolutely nothing going on in the tiny village below the coastal road from Ágios Nikólaos to Sitía. And that is the reason you came here: to sit in the few tavernas by the water, bathe at the tiny beach – and perhaps go over to the uninhabited *islet* right off the coast. All life focuses on the *platía* by the water, with a spot of sand and several tavernas.

If you haven't come to chill and read, you'll probably take a boat over to the island to see the excavations of a significant Minoan settlement by archaeologists from the University of North Carolina. The American archaeologist Richard Seager first broke the ground with spades here in 1908. The burial objects he excavated, including lovely gold jewellery, can now be seen in the museums at Iráklio, Ágios Nikólaos and Sitía. Work on the excavations was resumed in 1990. Go to one of the tavernas and ask about *the boatman who is usually available from 1 pm.* The only intact building on the island is the white *Chapel of St Nicolas.* Walk around the excavations, which have not yet been prepared for visitors, and you can look into several Minoan graves, see the remains of Roman settlements – including fish tanks – and traces of a Byzantine settlement. It's not particularly informative, but it's wildly romantic. Warning: Don't try to swim over to the island, as there are strong, unpredictable undercurrents. 🔲 S5

INSIDER TIP
Resist the temptation

The Faneroménis monastery is abandoned; icons now adorn a rock cave next door

DISCOVERY TOURS

Want to get under the skin of the region? Then our discovery tours provide the perfect guide – they include advice on which sights to visit, tips on where to stop for that perfect holiday snap, a choice of the best places to eat and drink and suggestions for fun activities.

❶ NATURE & HISTORY IN THE COUNTRYSIDE AROUND RÉTHIMNO

➤ Great spots lined up for you
➤ Hiking is a part of it
➤ A huge selection of souvenirs

📍	Réthimno	🏁	Réthimno
🔄	100 km	🚗	1 day (2½ hrs total driving time)
ℹ️	Take a torch for exploring the ancient cisterns.		

Crossing a stream at the bottom of the Samariá Gorge

VIA VENICE TO THE CRETAN NATIONAL SHRINE

You are advised to leave ❶ Réthimno ➤ p. 60 *via the old coastal road that runs east through the hotel quarter because there are no signs marking the improvised exit ramps on the motorway. In Plataniás, a well-marked road to Arkádi Monastery branches off from the coastal road. Shortly before you reach Ádele, take a little detour to the old Venetian village of* ❷ Marulás. A good portion of the historic houses here have been bought by foreigners and extensively renovated. Walk around the village for about a half an hour and then drive back to the main road. *As the road climbs upward, it passes through several villages and then through a narrow valley. Almost unexpectedly, you will finally come to the isolated* ❸ Arkádi Monastery ➤ p. 67, high up on a plateau. You should plan on spending about an hour looking around the most significant of the Cretan national shrines.

KEEPING YOUR EYE ON THE SUMMIT

An asphalt road leads from Arkádi Monastery east towards Eléftherna. At first, it still crosses over the plateau, offering picture-perfect views of Arkádi and the surrounding area from different points along the way. Drive

❶ **Réthimno**

10 km 10 mins

❷ **Marulás**

15 km 15 mins

❸ **Arkádi Monastery**

7 km 7 mins

through the desolate and barren maquis landscape, past grazing goats and sheep, before *taking the often empty road to the village of* ❹ Eléftherna. There are four quaint coffee houses in which at least a few chatty older gentlemen always seem to wait for new patrons to come in. The highest mountain on the island, Mount Psilorítis, can easily be seen from here to the southeast.

❹ Eléftherna

4 km   4 mins

ANCIENT CISTERNS

As you drive on, you will come to the neighbouring village of ❺ Archéa Eléftherna, which stands on the site of the significant ancient city of Eléftherna. Systematic excavations first began here in 1985. Every summer, researchers from the University of Crete continue to dig for artefacts. The best thing to do is drive from the village square down to the taverna *Akropolis* (€) and then set off on foot to explore the ancient ruins. A five-minute walk along the remains of the old city wall will bring you to two huge cisterns that were hewed into the rock about 2,300 years ago. You can explore them carefully if you have a torch. If you *continue along the path to the north for six or seven minutes, you will come to a terrace* where you'll find the excavated ruins of a

❺ Archéa Eléftherna

4 km   4 mins

INSIDER TIP
This way to antiquity

Watch potters transform sticky clay into beautiful vessels in Margarítes

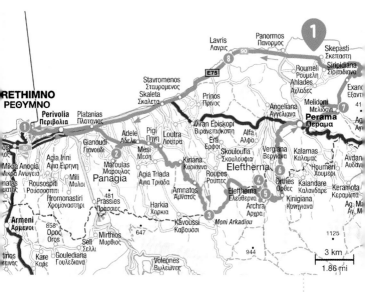

shrine of some kind beneath the old olive trees. This is the perfect place to enjoy a peaceful picnic accompanied by the natural music of the cicadas. You'll have to get back in the car to reach one of the other excavation areas of Eléftherna. *Follow the signs on the road to Margarítes that read "Ancient Eléftherna".* They will bring you to the remains of a Roman thermal bath and an early Christian Basilica.

AUTHENTIC FOOD & SHOPPING

❻ Margarítes ➤ p. 68 is the name of the next destina-
tion, which you should reach around 1 pm. *At the first potter's workshop on the right-hand side of the road*, you can watch as man-sized storage vessels are made right before your eyes. The Cretans call them *pithoi*. A number of other local potters sell clay creations that are easier to take home on a plane. The two tavernas on the village square in Margarítes are equally good and serve fantastic food. *The route continues downhill until you come to the old national road, which was the only link between Réthimno and Iráklio until the beginning of the 1980s. Turn right onto the national road in the direction of Pérama. When you get there, turn left*

❻ Margarítes

10 km   10 mins

7 Melidóni

18 km   18 mins

towards the coast. *You will rumble over a narrow bridge and then turn right just after the bridge* to head to **7** Melidóni. Shortly before you reach the village, you can stop on the right-hand side at the Paráskákis olive oil factory and buy some good oil to take home. *From the village square, you should drive another 2–3 km in the direction of Agía* because a number of charcoal kilns are fired here. Afterwards, the village square in Melidóni is a great place to take a break before driving up to the stalactite cave ➤ p. 68, which is another Cretan national memorial site.

SWIMMING AT SUNSET

Depart Melidóni and drive to the sleepy hamlet of Exándis. Turn right onto the road leading uphill to get to the new national road, which you will then take to the west. Expansive **8** Geropótamos Beach is the perfect spot for a swim as the sun sets over the Aegean. When it's time for dinner, head back to **1** Réthimno.

8 Geropótamos Beach

18 km   18 mins

1 Réthimno

2 QUIET VILLAGES BETWEEN THE AEGEAN & LIBYAN SEAS

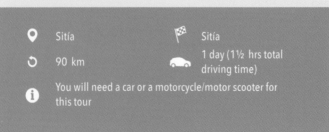

- ➤ See things very few people ever get to see
- ➤ Untouched nature abounds
- ➤ Swim in the Libyan Sea

📍	Sitía	🏁	Sitía
🔄	90 km	🚗	1 day (1½ hrs total driving time)
ℹ️	You will need a car or a motorcycle/motor scooter for this tour		

1 Sitía

25 km   25 mins

THROUGH DEEP VALLEYS

Depart **1** Sitía ➤ p. 118 and *head south, following the signs for Ierápetra. As soon as you get to Piskokéfalo, turn*

right onto the small road to Análipsi. After passing through Achládia, the road climbs up to the pass at Skordílo. In early summer, gorse seems to bloom everywhere. Later in the season, it looks like the rocky landscape has been blanketed with puffy pillows of green herbs. At the top of the pass, you will get your first glimpse of the Libyan Sea. *Drive down into the high valley* of ❷ Dafní, which is full of olive trees. *After you've left Dafní, you will come to another mountain valley further below*. In this area, you will see blocks of pure chalk lying on the side of the road. Get your creative juices flowing and draw a little picture on the road with one of the small pieces of chalk lying around. *As you drive on, you will come to the mouth of a valley* that runs from the

❷ Dafní

10 km   10 mins

north coast into the mountains. Storms often blow through this natural wind tunnel, shearing through the pine trees. Over the next few miles, you'll notice how the winds have cut the most bizarre, lopsided shapes into the trees. *Drive through Chrisopigí and pass by the totally isolated mountain village of Lápithos and make your next stop in* ❸ Stavrochóri. The particularly quaint *kafenío* on the through road is the perfect place for a long overdue coffee. *The road ends after another 35 km in the coastal village of* ❹ Koutsourás. Greenhouses have been built here right in the centre of the village – take a minute to inspect one of them up close.

HIKING ON NARROW TRACKS

Take the coastal road to the left and drive for just five minutes to ❺ Makrígialos ➤ p. 111. After a swim in the Libyan Sea, the small harbour is an excellent place to grab lunch. *Then, follow the main road east again. Just after Vóri, turn right and drive up to* ❻ Etía *and the village of* ❼ Chandrás. On this elevated plateau, where sultanas are the main crop, the pace of life is leisurely and the tourists are few and far between as you'll notice in the village *kafenía*. Once you are ready to leave this tranquillity behind, take a small detour from ❽ Néa Presós ➤ p. 126 to the meagre ruins of the ancient city of Presós on a hill. You can hike along the narrow paths to your heart's content with the most beautiful views of the Cretan mountains. *Late in the afternoon, drive north to get back to* ❶ Sitía.

INSIDER TIP
Lunch with a harbour view

❸ Stavrochóri

7 km   7 mins

❹ Koutsourás

3 km   3 mins

❺ Makrígialos

17 km   17 mins

❻ Etía

3 km   3 mins

❼ Chandrás

6 km   6 mins

❽ Néa Presós

17 km   17 mins

❶ Sitía

Nothing can beat real coffee when it is brewed with sugar and love in a brass jug

❸ THE BEAUTIFUL SURROUNDINGS OF THE COSTA TOURISTICA

➤ Unspoilt areas close to resorts
➤ Eat and drink in villages
➤ Swim in a fjord

📍	Ágios Nikólaos	🏁	Chersónisos
➡	100 km	🚗	1 day (2 ½ hrs total driving time)

ℹ Bring a torch to explore the cave
The **Palace of Mália** is only open until 3 pm

GREAT VIEWS & COFFEE IN THE SHADE

Follow the coastal road from ❶ Ágios Nikólaos ➤ p. 94 *northwards to Eloúnda and Pláka. Leave the coast behind and drive up to the mountain village of* ❷ Vroúchas. Enjoy the spectacular view of the fortress island of *Spinalónga* ➤ p 99. Keep driving through the countryside dotted with isolated small villages such as ❸ Káto Loúmas and ❹ Skiniás. If you find an open *kafenío*, stop for a drink – the locals will be surprised to see a tourist. *At the fork just after leaving Váltos, take the road to* ❺ Karídi. Shortly before you get to the village, you will spy a road to the left leading to the Aréti Monastery at a height of 530 m, which is worth a visit. In the 16th century, it once served as a bishop's residence. Today, only two monks sometimes live here. You can then enjoy a coffee break under a plane tree on the village square at ❻ Fourní ➤ p. 101 *before you continue along a eucalyptus-lined road to the neighbouring village of* ❼ Kastélli ➤ p. 101. Spend a quarter of an hour strolling through the pretty village, which has numerous Venetian buildings.

❶ Ágios Nikólaos	
20 km	20 mins
❷ Vroúchas	
4 km	4 mins
❸ Káto Loúmas	
4 km	4 mins
❹ Skiniás	
6 km	6 mins
❺ Karídi	
6 km	6 mins
❻ Fourní	
1 km	1 mins
❼ Kastélli	
6 km	6 mins

CAVE EXPLORATION

Drive through Nikithianó to 8 Neápoli, *and then follow the signs to Iráklio in order to get to Latsída. In the centre of the village, turn right and then just outside the village, turn left towards* 9 Kounáli. Stop for an excellent lunch along the main road on the shady terrace of the taverna To Kounáli *(€)* owned by a former ship's cook and his flower-crazy daughter. A bit of exercise will do you good after your meal. *On the curvy road between Kounáli and Mílatos, park your car and take a short walk to the* 10 Milátou stalactite cave *on the left-hand side. Don't forget a torch!* After exploring this subterranean world, *drive through Mílatos to arrive at* 11 Sísi ➤ p. 101 with its amazingly beautiful, although extremely short, fjord. For a cup of coffee or a refreshing drink, head to the Skipper Cocktail Bar directly above the fjord. If you feel like testing the water, there is a small sandy beach on the western end of the fjord where you can go for a swim.

FROM ANTIQUITY INTO THE WORLD OF FUN WATER PARKS

As you leave Sísi, follow the signs for Mália and Iráklio, which will bring you to the motorway. After about 2 km, follow the signs to the Minoan Palace of Mália ➤ p. 84. If you get there before it closes (3 pm), it's worth taking a look. If you're too late, you'll have to make do with a glimpse through the wire fence. You haven't wasted your time either way as the lovely beach and harbour of 12 Mália ➤ p. 84 are just a stone's throw away. If you walk *150 m to the west,* you can play a round of backgammon, Uno or Scrabble with Greek letters at the Snack Bar Blue Sea *(€).* Afterwards, *continue to the west on the old national road (avoid the motorway!) until you come to the resort of Stalída on the eastern edge of* 13 Liménas Chersónisou ➤ p. 82. It is home to the Star Beach Water Park ➤ p. 83 with its bungee crane and a variety of water-sports stations. How about a little parasailing adventure?

END THE DAY WITH A CRETAN EVENING

Drive into the town of Liménas Chersónisou and follow the signs for the village of 14 Koutouloufári, about half

a mile above the main town, where plenty of jewellery and handicrafts are on offer. For a late dinner, head to the village square of ⑮ Chersónisos ➤ p. 82. Every Monday, a folkloric "Cretan Evening" is held here.

⑮ Chersónisos

The Minoans chose premium locations for their palaces, at Knossós and Mália

❹ A SELF-GUIDED HIKE THROUGH CRETE'S MOST FAMOUS GORGE

➤ A challenge for hikers
➤ High peaks and steep rock faces
➤ Boat trip included

📍	Chaniá	🏁	Chaniá
↻	150 km	🥾	2 days (7–8 hrs total hiking time)
📶	medium		

ℹ️ It is essential to take water and sun protection. The gorge is only accessible from the beginning of May to 15 October. The last public bus from Chaniá departs at 8.45 am. Bus timetables: *e-ktel.com*; ferry timetables: *anendyk.gr*

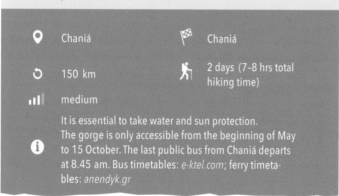

DAY 1
❶ Chaniá

37 km   37 mins

❷ Omalós Plateau

DAY 2

5 km   90 mins

❸ Samariá Gorge

400 m   2 mins

❹ Xylóskalo

7 km   2 hrs 15 mins

BRIGHT & EARLY INTO THE GORGE

Make sure you're on time to catch the bus from ❶ Chaniá ➤ p. 42 *up to* ❷ Omalós Plateau *because there is no later bus*. You will arrive around 10.30 am and then treat yourself to a refreshing day of relaxation at a height of over 1,000 m. Spend the night in the tranquil village of Omalós.

Start your hike through the gorge when it opens early the next morning at 7 am. This way, you will have already done most of the trail by the time the heat really intensifies at midday. *But first, you will have to walk about 5 km from your hotel in Ómalos along an asphalt road, unless your hotelier organizes rides, to reach the head of the* ❸ Samariá Gorge. *The actual trail begins a few steps further at a height of 1,229 m at the* ❹ Xylóskalo, *the wooden steps that bring you into the gorge*. Don't worry, though, because these are not actually stairs, but rather a pleasant forest path with steps here and there. Under the eyes of the Gíngilos (2,080 m), the trail wanders *for about an hour up through the forest to the floor of the gorge* through which a rushing stream flows. You will come to the abandoned village of **⑤ Samariá**, which has a freshwater spring, a first-aid station and toilets. The last residents left in 1962 when the gorge was turned into a national park.

THE SEA & A BOAT AWAIT AT THE FINISH LINE

As the trail continues, the gorge narrows steadily until you come to the so-called **⑥ Iron Gate (Sideróporta)**, *where it is only 3–4 m wide. Shortly thereafter, the coastal plain will appear before you, and then it is just another 3 km (without any shade) to the coastal hamlet of* **⑦ Agía Rouméli** with its many tavernas, guesthouses and a long pebble beach. The first thing you should do is buy your tickets for the ferry to Chóra Sfakíon. Then you can enjoy a long break in one of the tavernas and maybe a swim. The last ferry usually leaves around 5.30 pm, arriving at its destination about an hour later. In **⑧ Chóra Sfakion ➤ p. 55**, the public buses to Chaniá always wait for the ferry to dock. You should arrive back in **❶ Chaniá** around 8.30 pm

⑤ Samariá	
5.5 km	3 hr
⑥ Iron Gate	
2,5 km	45 mins
⑦ Agía Rouméli	
19 km	75 mins
⑧ Chóra Sfakíon	
70 km	70 mins
❶ Chaniá	

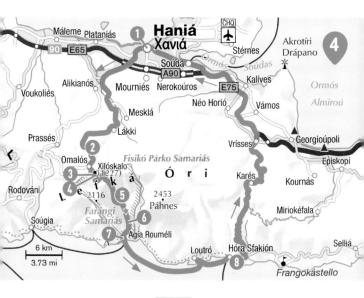

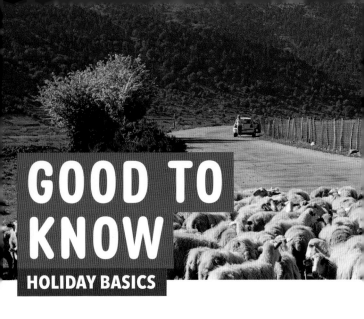

GOOD TO KNOW
HOLIDAY BASICS

ARRIVAL

+ 2 hours time difference

Crete is two hours ahead of Greenwich Mean Time, seven hours ahead of US Eastern Time and seven hours behind Australian Eastern Time.

GETTING THERE

There are daily flights to Crete all year with Olympic Air/Aegean Airlines *(www.aegeanair.com)*. Between Easter and October there are also many direct charter and budget flights directly to Iráklio and Chaniá but these can sometimes be more expensive than normal flights. Flights from London to Iráklio take about three and a half hours and from Athens about

40 minutes. At both airports there are taxis for further transport. At Chaniá and Iráklio there are also reasonably priced buses to the nearby city centre. Crete's third biggest airport in Sitía in eastern Crete receives domestic flights from Sky Express *(www.skyexpress.gr)*. Taxis are available at the arrival zone of the airport.

There is no direct ferry service from Italy. You have to cross to Patras on the Peloponnese first, then from Piraeus to Crete. There are daily ferries from Piraeus to Chaniá and Iráklio (6–12 hrs); several times a week to Réthimno and Sitía. There are also two to three ferries a week from Kissámos in the Peloponnese.

GETTING IN

You can travel to Greece without a visa so long as your stay does not exceed 90 days. If you intend to stay for longer, check which visa you require with the

Expect more sheep than tourists on the Omalós Plateau

Greek embassy. On arrival, your passport must have at least three months validity after your point of departure from Greece.

Electricity

You will need a UK–EU adapter for your devices.

CLIMATE & WHEN TO GO

Crete is not really a winter holiday destination. Between November and March it can rain and be quite cool. The best holiday months are from April to October. Swimming in the sea is best between May and November. May is the most beautiful time to travel in Crete: it is very green and there are flowers in bloom everywhere. It hardly rains from June to September; temperatures can reach 40°C and the average temperatures for July and August are 30°C by day and 20°C at night. There are also often strong winds on Crete that can even bring the ferries to a standstill for hours in the summer.

GETTING AROUND

BUSES

There are regular and 🐑 cheap public buses to almost every town in Crete and travelling by bus is recommended, since parking spaces are scarce. The blue buses only travel within municipal districts. Long-distance buses (often green) travel between Iráklio, Ágios Nikólaos, Chaniá, Ierápetra, Sitía and Réthimno. Tickets are bought in advance at the bus terminals in the cities; if you get on later, you buy the tickets from the driver. Tickets for city buses must be bought in advance at kiosks, hotel receptions and shops. Timetables for western Crete can be found at *e-ktel.com* and for eastern Crete at *ktelherlas.gr*.

CAR HIRE
Cars, motorbikes, Vespas and mopeds can be rented at all airports as well as in the towns and holiday resorts. Your national driving licence is sufficient proof of identity when booking. It is highly recommended to compare prices on the Internet. Usually, Greek rental firms hand the hire vehicle over with an almost empty tank. You are expected to return it in the same state and will not get a refund for excess petrol in the tank.

FERRIES
Ferries within Crete only sail along the south coast between Paleochóra and Chóra Sfakíon and also between the coastal towns in this region and the island of Gávdos. For schedules and prices please visit *anendyk.gr*.

ORGANISED TOURS
All holiday resorts and hotels offer organised excursions by bus or boat. Bus tours are usually accompanied by local and licensed guides. Gorge hikes and boat trips with transfer from the hotel to the harbour and back are often on the programme.

PLANES
There is only one route on the island of Crete and that is between Iráklio and Sitía, offered by *Sky Express (skyex press.gr)*. You can use it as a good sightseeing flight as the propeller-powered plane flies at low altitudes. You can also take the bus for your return journey.

INSIDER TIP Flightseeing!

ROAD TRAFFIC
The maximum speed in towns is 50 kmh and on national roads 90 kmh. Maximum blood alcohol level is 0.5. Right of way is not indicated as such. You will only recognise it by the 'Stop' and 'Give Way' signs in minor roads. At roundabouts, anything coming from the right has right of way, unless signposted otherwise. Cretans are notorious for cutting curves, so always keep to the right of the road. Also get used to honking at blind corners! During autumn, the roads are especially wet and slippery and care should be taken. Breakdown assistance can be obtained from the automobile club *ELPA*, country wide *tel. 1 04 00*. Car rental firms often have contracts with private recovery services.

TAXIS
Taxis are available in abundance and are not very expensive. Get one at the taxi rank or wave one down in the street. It is possible to book them in advance for a surcharge.

FESTIVALS & EVENTS
ALL YEAR ROUND

FEBRUARY/MARCH
Carnival Sunday (Réthimno) Large carnival procession and loud samba music with Greek lyrics.

MARCH/APRIL
Good Friday Processions in the evening everywhere, and in the big towns and cities also from the afternoon.
Easter Saturday Easter Mass from 11 pm (almost all Cretans go). Fireworks shortly after midnight.
Sunday after Easter Church service in the cave at Mílatos followed by free entertainment and refreshments on the village square by the sea.

JUNE
🚩 **Mátala Beach Festival** At Whitsun there are three days of open-air festivals in Mátala like the good old hippie days: *matalabeachfestival.org*

JULY
Dance Day (Chaniá) 12-day international festival of contemporary dance: *dancedays.gr*

JULY/AUGUST
Festival of Culture (Iráklio) All kinds of events, including open-air theatres: *heraklion.gr*

AUGUST
Over the Wall (Iráklio) Two days of an international rock festival, focusing on heavy metal. *overthewallfestival. com*
Potato Festival (Tzermiádo/Lassíthi Plateau) Music, dance, a fair and potatoes of all sorts. On the weekend after the 15 August.
🐟 **Houdétsi Festival** (near Iráklio) Four-day festival of Cretan music, admission free. *FB: Houdetsi Festival*

OCTOBER
Renaissance Festival (Réthimno) 12 days of concerts and theatre performances mostly in the castle. *rfr.gr*
Parish Festival (Gouvernétu Monastery near Chaniá) With a procession from the monastery to the cave for a festive service on 7 October.

EMERGENCIES

CONSULATES & EMBASSIES
British Vice Consulate Crete
17 Thalita | Ag. Dimitrios Sq. | Iráklio | tel. 28 10 22 40 12 | crete@fco.gov.uk

Canadian Embassy (Athens)
48 Ethnikis Antistaseos | 15231 Athens | tel. 21 07 27 34 00 | www.canada international.gc.ca/greece-grece

UK Embassy (Athens)
1 Ploutarchou | 10675 Athens | tel. 21 07 27 26 00 | ukingreece.fco. gov.uk

US Embassy (Athens)
91 Vasilissis Sophias | 10160 Athens | tel. 21 07 21 29 51 | gr.usembassy.gov

EMERGENCY SERVICES
Dial 112 for all emergency services: police, fire brigade and ambulance. The number is toll-free countrywide, and English is spoken.

HEALTH
Well-trained doctors guarantee basic medical care throughout Crete, however, there is often a lack of technical equipment. If you are seriously ill, it is advisable to return home; this will be covered by your travel insurance. Emergency treatment in hospitals is free of charge and you can be treated for free by doctors if you present the European Health Insurance Card issued by your own insurance company. However, in practice doctors do so reluctantly and it is better to pay cash, get a receipt and then present your bills to the insurance company for a refund.

Most towns and villages have chemists that are well stocked but they may not always have British medication.

ESSENTIALS

ACCOMMODATION
A large number of hotels, B&Bs, holiday apartments and homes are available not just in the towns and coastal resorts, but these days also in many of the mountain villages. Almost all accommodation providers are linked with the *booking.com* portal where you can get a good overview. You may of course be able to book directly with the landlord if that's any cheaper.

Camping anywhere other than a campsite is prohibited in Crete but is often done on isolated beaches. There are a total of 16 camping sites on the island that are open between April and October.

In Crete there are several simple accommodation units calling themselves "youth hostels" but none of them is a member of the international Youth Hostel Association. They are mostly privately owned. The only *"youth hostel"* worth recommending is the one in Plakiás.

BEACHES
Many beaches are only cleaned in front of hotels and where sun

loungers and parasols are for hire. Lifeguards are only to be found on highly frequented beaches and mainly during peak season. Seaweed that has been washed onto the beach at the beginning of the season is often only removed in May or June. Bathing shoes are recommended on many of the beaches (especially in summer when the sand tends to get extremely hot). Nude bathing is prohibited, but is practised on many isolated beaches. The only official nudist beach in Crete lies west of Chóra Sfakíon at the only nudist hotel in Greece, *Hotel Vritomártis*. Topless sunbathing is accepted everywhere.

CUSTOMS

EU citizens can import and export goods for their personal use tax-free (but only 800 cigarettes, 90 litres of wine, 10 litres of spirits). Visitors from other countries must observe the following limits, except for items for personal use. Duty free are: max. 50g perfume, 250 cigarettes, 50 cigars, 250g tobacco, 1 litre of spirits (over 22% vol.), 2 litres of spirits (under 22% vol.), 25 litres of any wine.

DRINKING WATER

You can drink the (chlorinated) tap water everywhere except Iráklio. Still mineral water *(metallikó neró)* is also available in restaurants and cafés and is usually the same price as in the supermarkets.

EARTHQUAKES

Light earthquakes do occur every once in a while and are no reason to panic. Should you experience an earthquake, take cover underneath a door frame, a table or a bed. As soon as the quake is over you should go outside (but do not use the lifts) and then stay clear of walls and flower pots that might topple over. Once outside follow the lead of the locals.

INTERNET & WIFI

Almost all hotels, bars, cafés and tavernas offer free wifi. Ask the waiter for the password.

LANGUAGE

The Greeks are very proud of their language characters which are unique to Greece. More and more place names are being written in Roman letters as well, but it is still helpful to have some knowledge of the Greek alphabet (see below). However, there is no uniform transliteration, so don't be surprised if you can encounter a place name in four different versions while you're in Crete.

GREEK ALPHABET

A	α	a	N	ν	n
B	β	v, w	Ξ	ξ	ks, x
Γ	γ	g, i	O	ο	o
Δ	δ	d	Π	π	p
E	ε	e	P	ρ	r
Z	ζ	s, z	Σ	σ, ς	s, ss
H	η	i	T	τ	t
Θ	θ	th	Y	υ	i, y
I	ι	i, j	Φ	φ	f
K	κ	k	X	χ	ch
Λ	λ	l	Ψ	ψ	ps
M	μ	m	Ω	ω	o

HOW MUCH DOES IT COST?

Boat tour	20 to 40 euros *all day, without transfer*
Coffee	1.50 to 3 euros *for an espresso/mocha*
Gyros	2.50 to 3 euros *for gyros and a pitta bread*
Wine	2.50 to 6 euros *for a glass of wine*
Petrol	1.70 euros *for a litre of unleaded petrol*
Deckchairs	6 to 10 euros *per day for two people including parasol*

Sometimes the correct accents on addresses, hotel and restaurant names are missing in this guide. The locals often don't know them anyway; they seldom call places by their official names and are used to calling hotels and tavernas according to the owner's name. When giving addresses, it is better to name landmarks rather than a street name.

MONEY & CREDIT CARDS

The national currency is the euro (pronounced ewró) and the cents are called *leptá*. Bank opening hours are Mon–Thu 8 am–2 pm, Fri 8 am–1.30 pm. You can withdraw money from many cash machines with your credit or debit card.

PHOTOGRAPHY

It might sound ridiculous given the large number of spy satellites orbiting the earth, but taking photographs of military installations is strictly prohibited and the respective signs must absolutely be observed. Over the years, quite a number of foreigners have spent many weeks behind bars because they were spotted taking pictures of military jets during take-off or landing.

POST

There are post offices in all cities and larger villages, open Mon–Fri 7 am–3 pm. In the tourism centres they sometimes open later in the afternoon as well as Saturday mornings.

PUBLIC HOLIDAYS

1 Jan	New Year's Day
6 Jan	Epiphany
Feb/March	Shrove Monday
25 March	Independence Day
March/April	Good Friday
March/April	Easter
1 May	Labour Day
Late May	Whitsun
15 Aug	Assumption Day
28 Oct	National holiday
25/26 Dec	Christmas

SHOP OPENING HOURS

In the resorts most shops open daily from 10 am to 11 pm. In the towns and cities, shops with a predominantly local customer base are open Mon–Sat at least 10 am–1.30 pm and Tue, Thu, Fri also from 5.30–8 pm.

SMOKING

The smoking ban is strictly observed on public transport and in airports, but it is given much more leeway in many cafés, tavernas and bars. On Crete, cigarettes are approximately one-third cheaper than in the UK, and non-filter cigarettes are also available.

TELEPHONE COUNTRY CODES

Greece *0030*
UK *0044*
United States *001*
Australia *0061*

TIPPING

Tips are only expected in very touristy places. Greeks tend to give too much sometimes rather than always too little; small tips under 50 cents are seen as an insult. Tips are left on the table when leaving.

TOILETS

Many of Crete's toilets can be very posh and equipped with the latest Italian sanitary installations; others should only be used in emergencies. Be aware that even in the good hotels you are not allowed to flush the used toilet paper down the drain, but have to throw it in the bin provided. The reason for this is that the paper clogs the often narrow drains and septic tanks.

TOURIST INFORMATION

Local tourist information offices (available in Ágios Nikólaos, Chaniá, Iráklio and Sitía) are often of little help and do not act as agents for accommodation or event tickets.

WEATHER

High season
Low season

	JAN	FEB	MARCH	APRIL	MAY	JUNE	JULY	AUG	SEPT	OCT	NOV	DEC
Daytime temperatures (°C)	16°	16°	17°	20°	24°	28°	30°	30°	27°	24°	21°	17°
Night-time temperatures in (°C)	9°	9°	10°	12°	15°	19°	21°	22°	19°	16°	14°	11°
Sunshine hours/day	3	5	6	8	10	12	13	12	10	6	6	4
Rainy days/month	12	7	8	4	2	1	0	0	2	6	6	10
Sea temperatures in °C	16	15	16	16	19	22	24	25	24	23	20	17

☀ Sunshine hours/day   🐦 Rainy days/month   ≈ Sea temperatures in °C

USEFUL WORDS & PHRASES

SMALLTALK

Yes/no/maybe	ne/ˈochi/ˈissos	Ναι/ Όχι/Ισως
Please/Thank you	parakaˈlo/efcharisˈto	Παρακαλώ/ Ευχαριστώ
Good morning/good evening/goodnight!	kalliˈmera/kalliˈspera/ kalliˈnichta!	Καλημέραμ/ Καλησπέρα!/ Καληνύχτα!
Hello/ goodbye (formal)/ goodbye (informal)!	ˈya (su/sass)/ aˈdio/ ya (su/sass)!	Γεία (σου/σας)!/ αντίο!/Γεία (σου/ σας)!
My name is …	me ˈlene …	Με λένεÖ …
What's your name?	poss sass ˈlene?	Πως σας λένε?
Excuse me/sorry	me sigˈchorite/ sigˈnomi	Με συγχωρείτε / Συγνώμη
Pardon?	oˈriste?	Ορίστε?
I (don't) like this	Afˈto (dhen) mu aˈressi	Αυτό (δεν) ουμ αρέσει

SYMBOLS

EATING & DRINKING

Could you please book a table for tonight for four?	Klis'te mass parakal'lo 'enna tra'pezi ya a'popse ya 'tessera 'atoma	Κλείστε ασμ παρακαλώ ένα τραπέζι γιά απόψε γιά τέσσερα άτοαμ
The menu, please	tonn ka'taloggo parakal'lo	Τον κατάλογο παρακαλώ
Could I please have ... ?	tha 'ithella na 'echo ...?	Θα ήθελα να έχο ...?
more/less	pjo/li'gotäre	ρπιό/λιγότερο
with/without ice/ sparkling	me/cho'ris 'pa-go/ anthrakik'ko	εμ/χωρίς πάγο/ ανθρακικό
(un)safe drinking water	(mi) 'possimo nä'ro	(μη) Πόσιμο νερό
vegetarian/allergy	chorto'fagos/allerg'ia	Χορτοφάγος/ Αλλεργία
May I have the bill, please?	'thel'lo na pli'rosso parakal'lo	Θέλω να πληρώσω παρακαλώ

MISCELLANEOUS

Where is ...?	pu tha vro ...?	Που θα βρω ...?
What time is it?	Ti 'ora 'ine?	Τι ώρα είναι?
How much does... cost ?	Posso 'kani ...?	Πόσο κάνει ...?
Where can I find internet access?	pu bor'ro na vro 'prosvassi sto índernett?	Που πορώμ να βρω πρόσβαση στο ίντερνετ?
pharmacy/ chemist	farma'kio/ ka'tastima	Φαρακείομ/ Κατάστημαμ καλλυντικών
fever/pain /diarrhoea/ nausea	piret'tos/'ponnos/ dhi'arria/ana'gula	Πυρετός/Πόνος/ Διάρροια/Αναγούλα
Help!/Watch out! Be Careful	Wo'ithia!/Prosso'chi!/ Prosso'chi!	Βοήθεια!/Προσοχή!/ Προσοχή!
Forbidden/banned	apa'goräfsi/ apago'räwäte	Απαγόρευση/ απαγορεύεται
0/1/2/3/4/5/6/7/8/9/ 10/100/1000	mi'dhen / 'enna / 'dhio / 'tria / 'tessera / 'pende /'eksi/ ef'ta/ och'to / e'nea / dhekka / eka'to / 'chilia / 'dhekka chil'iades	ηδενμ/ένα/δύο/τρία/ τέσσερα/πέντε/έξι/ εφτά/οχτώ/ εννέα/ δέκα/εκατό/χίλια/ δέκα χιλιάδες

HOLIDAY VIBES
FOR RELAXATION & CHILLING

FOR BOOKWORMS & FILM BUFFS

ZORBA THE GREEK

A Cretan classic, (both book and film) written by Níkos Kazantzákis and directed by Michael Cacoyannis in 1964, starring Anthony Quinn and Irene Pappas. It created the archetypal Cretan and still radiates a strong feeling of Cretan *joie de vivre.*

THE ISLAND

This historical novel by award-winning author Victoria Hislop is set on the former leper colony of Spinalónga, an island off the Cretan coast.

HE WHO MUST DIE

A 1956 film directed by Jules Dassin based on the novel *Christ Recrucified* by Níkos Kazantzákis and filmed mainly in Krítsa. It starred Melina Mercouri and Gert Fröbe. The topic has become current again: the plight of migrants.

THE DARK LABYRINTH

Lawrence Durrell didn't only write about Corfu. This captivating novel is set on Crete just after World War II, when a variety of English cruise-ship passengers come ashore to explore, with dramatic consequences.

PLAYLIST

0:58

II XYLOURIS WHITE – DAPHNE
Cretan *lýra* player George Xylouris and Australian drummer Jim White combine Cretan music with rock and free jazz.

▶ **PSARANTONIS & PSARONIKOS – O DIAS**
Brothers Antónis and Níkos Xylouris are regarded as the grand masters of Cretan *lýra* music.

▶ **ROSS DALY – EROTOKRITOS**
This Irishman who lives on Crete is a traditional musician who has developed his very own version of the *lýra*.

▶ **ADAEIS – NTROPI**
This band, founded in Iráklio in 2015, plays only rock music with Greek lyrics.

▶ **NANA MOUSKOURI – THE WHITE ROSE OF ATHENS**
The global star was born in Chaniá.

Your holiday soundtrack can be found on **Spotify** under **MARCO POLO** Greece

Or scan this code with the Spotify app

ONLINE

CRETE TV
Many films made in and featuring Crete and streamed live around the clock on cretetv.gr.

CRETAN BEACHES
This app describes more than 300 beaches on the island in great detail (in English).

HERSONISSOS LIFE
Are you wondering what to do tonight? This app gives recommendations on how to spend the evening in the best clubs on Crete (in English).

MY CRETE GUIDE
Best-rated travel app for Crete, with personalised information across 40 categories, including the E4 hiking trail. For Android, free.

LIVING IN CRETE
Website about expat life on Crete: livingincrete.net

GREEK MYTHOLOGY
Website (www.greekmythology.com) and app (for iOS and Android) all about the Greek myths, including specific information about the stories based on Crete.

TRAVEL PURSUIT
THE MARCO POLO HOLIDAY QUIZ

Do you know your facts about Crete? Here you can test your knowledge of the little secrets and idiosyncrasies of the island and its people. You will find the correct answers in the footer and in detail on pages 18 to 23 of this guide.

❶ What was Istanbul called in medieval times?
a) Erdoganobul
b) Konstantinoupolis
c) Ankara

❷ Wat is the name of Crete's best known musical instrument?
a) Lýra
b) Bagpipe
c) Harmonica

❸ What do Cretans call their national alcoholic drink?
a) Oúzo
b) Sambucca
c) Rakí

❹ Who killed the minotaur in the labyrinth?
a) Theseus
b) Paulus
c) Tsípras

❺ What is the Greek name for a taxi?
a) Entáxi
b) Taxí
c) Dolmus

❻ Who did queen Pasiphae fall in love with?
a) An Athenian prince
b) A white bull
c) Demis Roussos

An authentic Cretan evening: eating in good company while listening to live *lýra*

❼ What are greenhouses on the island made of?
a) Plastic
a) Lego bricks
a) Glass

❽ What do Cretans mean by "paréa"?
a) A piece of clothing
a) A group of companions
a) A parasol

❾ What are the Greek-Orthodox priests called?
a) Pharaos
b) Pristerádes
c) Pappádes

❿ Who was Aristotle?
a) A politician
b) A story-teller
c) A philosopher

⓫ Which tattoos are popular on Crete?
a) The 1-Euro coin
b) A spartan warrior
c) Alexis Sorbás

⓬ Which period of British history coincides with the Byzantine era?
a) The Middle Ages
b) Bronze age
c) Classical period

⓭ A popular Greek television comedy depicts whom as deadly?
a) Sons-in-law
b) Mothers-in-law
c) Grandmothers

⓮ What is the meaning of the Greek word "Ágia"?
a) A church
b) A square
c) A female saint

INDEX

WE WANT TO HEAR FROM YOU!

Did you have a great holiday? Is there something on your mind? Whatever it is, let us know! Whether you want to praise the guide, alert us to errors or give us a personal tip – MARCO POLO would be pleased to hear from you.

We do everything we can to provide the very latest information for your trip. Nevertheless, despite all of our authors' thorough research, errors can creep in. MARCO POLO does not accept any liability for this. Please contact us by e-mail.

e-mail: sales@heartwoodpublishing.co.uk

Picture credits
Cover: Crete, taverna at Chóra Sfakíon (huber-images: K. Kreder)
Photographs: K. Bötig (155); DuMont Bildarchiv: T. Gerber (56/57), Modrow (146), Spitta (128/129); huber-images: Mehlig (14/15), R. Schmid (45, 46, 72/73, 90/91, 121), A. Serrano (19), G. Simeone (66/67); huber-images/SIME: R. Spila (124/125); Laif: T. Gerber (35, 60, 64, 69, 81, 85, 86/87, 89, 96, 100/101, 108, 113, 122, 130, 134, 137), C. Heeb (78, 80, 104/105), C. Kerber (71), D. Schwelle (11); Laif/hemis: F. Guiziou (114/115); Laif/hemis.fr: J.-P. Degas (20, 26/27), B. Gardel (32/33); Laif/Le Figaro Magazine: Fabre (53); Laif/robertharding: T. Auzins (6/7, 12/13, 24/25), S. Black (48/49, 140/141), N. Farrin (77); mauritius images: Hackenberg (51), Tschanz-Hofmann (31); mauritius images/Alamy (23, 28, 38/39, 42), D. Crossland (118), R. Dziewulski (68), G. B. Evans (62), B. Forenius (10), A. McAulay (Klappe vorn außen), H. Milas (111), A. Mroszczyk (8), I. Tichonow (Klappe innen/1), J. Tregelles (143); mauritius images/a-plus image bank/Alamy (30/31); mauritius images/Delphotos/Alamy (54); mauritius images/Hackenberg-Photo-Cologne/Alamy (127); mauritius images/imagebroker: M. Breuer (94); mauritius images/imagebroker/gourmet-vision (27); mauritius images/John Warburton-Lee: K. Kreder (152/153); mauritius images/World Pictures (98); picture alliance/DUMONT Bildarchiv (9, 103); O. Stadler (2/3, 150/151)

4th Edition – fully revised and updated 2022
Worldwide Distribution: Heartwood Publishing Ltd, Bath, United Kingdom
www.heartwoodpublishing.co.uk

© MAIRDUMONT GmbH & Co. KG, Ostfildern
Author: Klaus Bötig; **Editor**: Christina Sothmann
Picture editor: Stefanie Wiese
Cartography: © MAIRDUMONT, Ostfildern (pp. 336-37, 131, 133, 137, 139, back cover, pull-out map); © MAIRDUMONT, Ostfildern, using map data from OpenStreetMap, Lizenz CC-BY-SA 2.0 (pp. 40–41, 45, 58–59, 63, 74–75, 79, 92–93, 97, 106–107, 116–117, 120).
Cover design and pull-out map cover design: bilekjaeger_Kreativagentur mit Zukunftswerkstatt, with Zukunftswerkstatt, Stuttgart; **page designs**: Langenstein Communication GmbH, Ludwigsburg

Heartwood Publishing credits:
Translated from the German by Thomas Moser, Wendy Barrow, Susan Jones, Jennifer Walcoff Neuheiser and Mo Croasdale
Editor: Felicity Laughton
Prepress: Summerlane Books, Bath
Printed in India

MARCO POLO AUTHOR
KLAUS BÖTIG

A well-known and prolific travel author on Greece, Klaus Bötig has a deep affinity to this land and its people. He much prefers to spend time with farmers in an olive grove making rakí at sunrise than putting on a tie for dinner in a distinguished restaurant. After decades of exploration on extensive trips, he still finds something new every single day – for you to discover while touring the beautiful island of Crete.

DOS & DON'TS

HOW TO AVOID SLIP-UPS & BLUNDERS

DO BE CAREFUL WHEN ORDERING FISH

Fresh fish and shellfish are expensive and often sold by weight. Always ask for the kilo price first and when the fish is being weighed, make sure you are present to avoid any unpleasant surprises on the bill.

DON'T DRIVE OFF-ROAD

If you are travelling with a hired vehicle and leave the main road, you will be driving without insurance and will have to pay for any damages yourself. That sometimes even goes for 4 × 4 vehicles! Tyre damage is not insured most of the time, even if the damage occurred on a tarmac road.

DON'T RISK A FOREST FIRE

The risk of a forest fire on Crete is high. Smokers must be especially careful and should never discard their cigarette butts. Broken glass can also ignite a fire.

DON'T COLLECT YOUR OWN SOUVENIRS

On the beach and in the mountains, no one will mind if you collect a pebble or two, but taking a stone that has been crafted into something or ceramic shards from an archaeological site is a criminal offence.